CW00460405

By the same author
A Strange Girl in Bright Colours
Unplayed Music
Star Whisper
Direct Dialling

as editor
Making for the Open:
The Chatto Book of Post-Feminist Poetry 1964–1984

Selected Poems

CAROL RUMENS

Chatto & Windus LONDON

Published in 1987 by
Chatto & Windus Ltd
30 Bedford Square
London WC1B 3RP

All rights reserved. No part of this publication may
be reproduced, stored in a retrieval system, or
transmitted in any form, or by any means,
electronic, mechanical, photocopying, recording or
otherwise, without the prior permission of
the publisher.

British Library Cataloguing in Publication Data
    Rumens, Carol
    Selected Poems.
    I. Title
    821'.914   PR6068.U6

ISBN 0-7011-3201-9

Copyright © Carol Rumens 1973, 1981, 1983, 1985, 1987

Typeset at The Spartan Press Ltd
Lymington, Hants
Printed in Great Britain by
Redwood Burn Ltd
Trowbridge, Wilts

ACKNOWLEDGEMENTS

'Sappho' first appeared in a pamphlet published by Ulsterman Publications
in 1978, *A Necklace of Mirrors*. 'Denunciation' first appeared in a
pamphlet, *Scenes from the Gingerbread House*, published by Bloodaxe
Books in 1982. *Icons, Waves* was published as a pamphlet by Star Wheel
Press in 1986.

Acknowledgements are also due to the following publications in which
some of the poems first appeared:

*Ambit, Aquarius, Encounter, Honest Ulsterman, Literary Review, The
London Review of Books, New Criterion, New Statesman, The Observer,
Outposts, Oxford Poetry, Poetry* (Chicago), *Poetry Book Society Supple-
ment* 1986, *PN Review, Stand, The Times Literary Supplement.*

CONTENTS

to my mother
and in memory of my father

Local Boy Makes Good

Justin, Prince of Poplar,
the fantasist in the fruit-salad shirt,
a destiny on his mind,
and the Cotton Street washing-girl
he lived with a year,
still in there, watering
the floor he shouldn't have stepped on
with his dirty dreams
big as fruit-machines,
and his disgust;
Justin of the docklands,
boarding a sun-bound bus,
taking off from Blackwater Basin, the cranes,
tenements and masts
reeling like Ferris wheels
as he sweats it out in the cockpit
of his jet-set acumen, schooled
never to look down
into the storms of laughter
and the white-face wind:
Justin Adamant,
lifeman of one mind,
who laughed off every crisis,
having taught himself the simple sum
– that in Cotton Street, tinned peas
cost dear, but in Wasserman's
of Piccadilly, West One,
there are pure silk bedspreads, prices
slashed by more than half.

The Star is Dead. Long Live the Superstar

The gods have bounced around the world,
jet-plane to Rolls and up again

— now they've dropped at your feet, give them a big hand.
Who needs Jesus, King of the Ravers,

who needs Krishna, who need Lucifer,
Dionysus, Moses, the Kamikaze?

These four make enough noise for the lot of them.
They are sprawling in the air,

nevertheless, pretending to be crucified,
the strobes hurling stained-glass

mythologies over the taut white faces.
Yes, this is the old religion, good as new,

coming on with acoustic miracles,
the snapped string a sacred sign,

the wild dances a raising of the lame.
The roadies may sweat, scurrying between wires

to soothe and adjust currents as high-strung
as their idols' souls, but the little girls

never get tired. They are burning
everlastingly. Their hair spins like fan-wheels.

Meanwhile, the drummer is attacking himself,
attacking and attacking.

The battered molecules, trying frantically
to recover their shape, must see that he's obsessed,

his blood torrential, his stance impossible.
On the backs of cymbals, snares, octa-plus tom-toms,

he rides through the hammer and stirrup of his nightmare
and is hurled among showers of disintegrating tin

onto a dud trip called being human.
Death fixes him, white-eyed, from the bedside glass,

but the fiery acolytes keep dancing;
they shake the drops from their eyes and understand

that even before the first flame has licked
the box and its flower-load, a smiling resurrection

will be at the vacant drum-kit, announcing itself:
the star is dead – long live the superstar!

Aesthetics

Caught off-guard by the impudent laser-beam,
alienated by a delicate whim,
the new aesthetes excitedly prospect
with guide-books and credit-cards the age of steam.

It is September. On warm holidays
when the West End flickers into humanity,
Pre-Raphaelite silks float sandalled feet,
and the subways speed enlightened coteries

seeking the dim hives of market stalls
where a Renaissance glory emanates
from the bland patina of Victorian industry
– daguerrotype, ivory, willow-pattern plate.

Meanwhile the 'mystic orient' sustains
Victorian travellers' tales. Its trinkets tipped
onto white cloth by a staring Tamil sell
competitively to the sadhus of SE6.

And the great Hampstead violinist pays
his private guru, forgotten in Bombay.

Obsessed, they shape the lineaments of world peace
through many a 'finely imagined phrase'.

Now Blackhill Enterprises close the last
festival marquee. The butterfly falls.
Though money sets ideals in perfect glaze
and transcribes the glamour of old movie-stars

into a not-quite-accurate verbatim,
the microbe of death navigates deeper mud
than the epidermis. Science hangs her head
when the beautiful die; she can only donate a post mortem.

At Puberty

After rain
a blue light settled over the convent arches.

The naked asphalt astonished itself with diamonds.
Even the exhausted plaster virgin
in the Bernadette Grotto and the mulberry tree,
propped up, and barren of silkworms,
stepped cleanly out of their decay.

From the back of the music lesson,
a girl stared through a window,
watching beam upon beam of realisation
incise the long mist of her childhood.

Komm liebe Mai
sang the class, uneasily.
A new emotion,
innocent, classical,
yet making her blush and burn
was softly unravelled
by the clear-eyed woman who sat

at the black Bösendorfer
with her coquettishness and her merciless,
gentle arpeggios.

The elm-leaves turned, silver-backed,
on a wind coarse as hunger.

And nuns in their distant sanctuary,
the dark-blue brides of Christ,
closed their ears to the sin, the soft,
tired alto of girls at puberty;
heard still a child's soprano.

O impossible miracles, light
out of straggle-rowed chairs
and school-room floorboards!

The girl, pale as clouds,
stares for a year

at the vision which cannot see
the speechless peasant,

which will suddenly vanish, leaving
only an enormous grief
like a deep river between them

– the woman who needed nothing
and the child who promised everything.

Remembering Morning Prayers

Salve Regina, in honour of your feast
we'll etch our knees with wood-grain, red and white
– cricks in the back, and indifference in the soul.
Will she, the pasteboard queen, attend our sighs,

as, blue on blue, the sulky armies drop

like thunder-claps, worn sandals tipped in pairs?
My eyes grip hard her mortal surfaces,
or close on venial thoughts. Her mysteries

lie somewhere else, the points of seven swords
shining with all her glory and dismay,
until the supernatural fainting-fit
in which she was assumed to rosy sky.

Alone, I saw her tears, and felt the quake
of innocent blood out of the torn heart.
But here, even the martyrs yawn. Beneath
the shoals of virgin coughs I drift awake.

Poor, faceless mother, voice a patter of beads,
form lashed to rocks and walls, helplessly bent
to those who drown, these pious headaches slip
through history now. What blessings came, are spent.

Magnificat

Snow-heaps cloud our glass-panelled door
like breath. On stereo,
the clear D major of '*Et exsultavit*'
branches and flows, is happiness without question,
that finds in itself, at length, a sharp enigma.
And abruptly, without trace,
the angel who danced between the casual ear
and the travelling stylus has flown
from the dust-collecting voice, embalmed in its groove.
Not even the first sun-shaft, the D major
commonplace, could hold him.
But perhaps beyond this door, this garden of glitters,
in the flat wastes where vandals
have uprooted the phones and twisted
the swings into child-scorning ideograms,

his echoes brush reality.
Such acts are unpitying
like the rape of the little Jewess
who can't have wanted to be anyone's mother
so early in her day.
They wound and illuminate
like a change of key, the dark question-mark
of the interrupted cadence.
The snow cannot hide them in its ordinariness,
but only lies back and stares. Hating such mischief,
the houses, spaced like primary triads,
push their chorales to the sky, but are not heard.

Houses by Day

Houses by day have silent insides.
They are solitude illuminated,
their spiders motionless, their dust intact.

I have lived here an impenetrable year,
with only a mirror to smile at, and a hot-water system
for an echo. I can just remember

an earlier daylight, a taller house,
sliced into dank flats, the landlord always away.
His pinched rooms glowed on our pioneer emotions.

It was the high mid-sixties;
wine bottles hogged the fireplace and lust flamed,
the Beatles louder than the repetitive wallpaper

when I woke in our junk-shop double bed
from a broken dream to an indissoluble law.
The tight ring dragged on my thickening finger.

The trauma of marriage swallowed me. I became

a ghost whose buried rage hoists furniture,
whose stultified self rattles in the attic.

Adjusted now, I have learned my role is to wait
for the key in the lock, to serve the first, clean kiss,
and light up at a flick of my clitoris.

A Future

The lights of the estate blink on at dusk
— little well-drilled municipals, one for each

porch. Through curtained panes, block after block,
the violet shadows flash

animus of some small-screen homicide.
Out in the real night, bottles are cracked

for real fights, real wounds. I can't escape,
nor can my children, making what the world

would call an ignominious beginning,
their landscape crowded, graceless and cut-price.

Fingers in mouths, they sleep beyond despair.
Toys colour at dawn. A new snow spills

its innocent stars over the pointed hoods
of anoraks shoving into the High Street where

plate-glass defines the limits of free will.
Sweets for the unsweet. I take, and share

the sugar gems, souring my children's teeth
in lieu of their inheritance. I weep.

Though no one's starving, and the poorest will
receive his little spring

by courtesy of the state and Montessori
– paints and clay, milk and imagination –

the landlord holds the clock's trump-card. These hopes
he'll blot, despite all miracles but money,

and money he'll withhold against all odds.
The rooms are shrinking fast, the colours die.

With snow-clogged boots the bailiff wanders in,
talks to the baby, comments on the cold,

nearly apologetic. It is fate.
The price-tagged dreams fall to the darkening street.

Eviction

His wife, rising at dawn, rock-brown, unspeaking;
his knife, African moon-sliver, baring its backbone;
his dread, reaching out into the morning.

The morning: simple, terrible, dead-white morning;
noise of his children and the clean-eyed baby;
his wife, sugaring whiteness for the feeder.

The jobless years, deserts of unused time;
dead bed where he hunched, trying to smoke out
the dread that always pointed to this morning.

The quick thrill of the doorbell, the banging,
the tramping into the hall, the thick, flushed faces
of the well-employed, the state assassins.
His wife on the stairs, bringing the filled white feeder.

How he jumped then, apathy behind him,
the years' beached bed-sheets like a sloughed-off skin;
how the knife flexed in his hand. It skimmed her morning

off-guard. She swore once, softly. Blood
flowered on her hand. The children screamed
at a fate worse than the bailiffs, their mother dying.

Panic. Panic and calm. The slow icing
of two astonished faces. Halted steps.
Sharp as an animal, he made for the bedroom,

saw nothing there to deflect, to pacify,
no trace of pity, all hope soused out
in light and screams and a sheaf of official papers.

He worked decisively in the upstairs room.
The darkness of his children,
tear-brilliant, poured into the open street.

Footsteps warned. His wife with her torn hand
had snatched the baby, bloodying its cries.
His throat became a mouth, the red words falling,

the knife falling, the sun falling. His dread
reached out its claw, and fixed each wavering child
to the white vice, the millstone of the morning.

Elegy

This is a summer of heat but no light,
the dim gardens uninhabited at dusk
that drifts pale blue and slightly smoke-soiled,
holding little hope of one ripe star.

Only Beech House slowly electrifies,
its windows coloured screens on a light-box module.
If you turned enough dials, would marvellous rainbows
    flow?
No, these are simply room-lights; distant specks

move, eat and die in them.
Generations of lives, they are stockpiled here
or set in rows behind the angular porchways
of Foxcombe and Applegarth, the bulldozed woodlands.

These are the stone fields where the poor are seeded
by random bureaucratic winds.
If they fail to root, there are priests and a welfare service:
no need to cut throats, scream, jump off balconies.

But the summer breeds its own ills. Each night
smashed glass chimes the hour, and wishes bleed
down walls autographed by the nameless young,
spilling their small fire into a granite tundra.

Inheritors

The street-lights bronze the pale weatherboard
house-fronts. Beyond their heads, twelve bald
bulbs climb one behind the other
up Beech House, beechless as Buchenwald.

Plimsolls pound. A human shadow drops
and coils for cover behind the concrete stair.
The panda car is watching somewhere else.
The broken glass winks under the star.

Outside the fish-shop, knives are flashed.
Down in the play-park, five
girls curse and laugh and jounce the metal horse,
and wait all evening to be snatched alive.

These are the locks they'll wake behind, and these
hard sons the sort they'll struggle not to raise
against the weatherboard and echoing stair,
down the cul-de-sacs as short as days.

One Street Beyond

From first light to pub time,
always the trackless children
skirmishing, sliding
through the grit of empty underpasses;
making a chase-game,
throwing coke-cans, threats,
tumbling down the absurd
grass flanks of the main road.
All day you hear them,
tractors and go-carts squealing
in mindless circles.
All day, some are clambering,
stranded on one
rusting climbing-frame.
Some are running away,
and others, standing staring
at a vacant play-space.
All through the long August
they are darkening, hardening
– the outdoor children
whose fathers come and leave
in vans or on foot
without a word;
whose mothers are always tired
and shouting from windows.
Making little, barbed worlds
from broken glass and match-sticks
at the edges of kerbs,
the children never listen.
They started with white socks,
new toys, washed faces,
but always end here,
dirty and alone,

one street beyond
justice or love.

Distinctions

The green hill-spine bends
to the new development
where graduates raise tulips and two
denimed kids apiece
in stucco semis; their
Condé Nast living-areas in glass cases swarm
along the poppy-field (kept
by a rustic whim), begin
to claw that gravelly scoop
borrowed from the hill,
and leased to artists all last summer. Strange
happenings of smoke-bombs, clowns,
masques and kinetic painting
brought down the TV cameras, and the odd
police-car, light buzzing, a throttle of rage,
before the sightseers revved and tutted away
up the dirt road. I
walked it every night,
padding on secretive soles the miles between
July poetry-readings in fierce sunlight,
and late September blues, enclosed,
under a skull of rain.
I came and listened, crouching, uneasy.
I didn't belong
to either sect, whose sparse lords balefully glared
at each other across the sandy floors
as night fell. The poppies dripped away.
Taking their bits of poems in plastic bags
and flowered vans full of mattresses,

pale girls and boys pitched camp.
The residents lowered their blinds,
smiled, and turned the switch marked apathy.
Again I climbed the hill
to where the old estate in scabby mounds
of rented concrete hangs.
It has no artistry, no wiles
but those of subsistence.
Its girls, with sober headscarves and great prams,
shove for their lives.

Night Song

A day of footloose sweetness, disenchanted
already – it begins to travel on.
The free can't keep from their double-locked apartments.
The city's watch-dogs can't detain the sun.

Outlawed, I gather up the words we dropped,
strain faded smiles from bottles left half-drunk
– garbage of memories, cleansed, assembled, loved,
to challenge this city's boredom, this room's dark.

Though time's barbed wall divides our continents,
wired to my desperate hunger, you return,
melting its shadows. Now the city lights
rise like the sun. Dream-trapped all night, we burn.

Lost Things

Red abdomen pulsing,
mouth opening, opening on naked air,
he perches in the astonishment of his change
– tiny, transparent frog –

half-tail'd still, and quick to return to the water,
his breast-stroke delicate, perfect;
but surfacing later, more boldly,
and, when nobody's watching,
suddenly leaping out to a lost life
somewhere in our back-garden, street, city.
Shrivelled by towering stone,
foot-snap or black squeeze of tyre,
he is meaningless in death, his seven weeks
of intricate life dulled to a clumsy joke.
I must not pity him. Let him become
as distant to me as newsreel refugees
poking about in small bowls, blind to the cameras.
They are all nature's expendables, a common clockwork
undone in seconds. To search
for soul or self, god-spark in every life,
was the last human myth.
The eye that counted hairs and the fall of sparrows
fails, is not even I, but a million i's,
leaping at dreams, dying in endless hunger.

Menopause

No pains, no midwife now;
this is the dud season
set between extremes
when the travel agent prints

red skies, gold skins
on the flat eye of the future.
It shuts. A woman mounts
her ageing escalator,

treading the rutted years
for music, like a stylus.

She catches, catches.
Her body glides by

on a pitiless turntable.
The light drops from her hands
to another latitude
where thin girls laugh

in the fumey slip-stream,
their lives blowing outwards.
This way, please, this way.
Here is a wooden cold,

a night unfit for journeys,
a night for turning home.
It is the twelfth month.
No baby cries.

Unplayed Music

We stand apart in the crowd that slaps its filled glasses
on the green piano, quivering her shut heart.
The tavern, hung with bottles, winks and sways
like a little ship, smuggling its soul through darkness.
There is an arm flung jokily round my shoulders,
and clouds of words and smoke thicken between us.
I watch you watching me. All else is blindness.

Outside, the long street glimmers pearl.
Our revellers' heat steams into the cold
as fresh snow, crisping and slithering
underfoot, witches us back to childhood.
Oh night of ice and Schnapps, moonshine and stars,
how lightly two of us have fallen in step
behind the crowd! The shadowy white landscape
gathers our few words into its secret.

All night in the small grey room
I'm listening for you, for the new music
waiting only to be played; all night I hear nothing
but wind over the snow, my own heart beating.

Akhmatova in Leningrad

Queuing at the gate of the Kresty,*
The whole city hanging in ice
Like jet beads in a paper-weight,
The woman turned to me twice

*The Leningrad jail where women queued daily,
hoping for news or a glimpse of imprisoned relatives.

As if to convince herself
It was mine, this wrecked white face,
Mine too, the song that had measured
Her hopes in warmer days.

The second time her voice
Was like the first seeping of spring
Wrung from the snow-blue lips
Of a mountainous sorrowing.

'Can you write about this?'
She opened her hand to the wall,
To the women, mute, as if
They queued for the price of a star.

She dropped her hand, she shrugged.
Locked out, I tried to guess
If I'd given her bread or a stone
In the burning clasp of my 'yes'.

Death of Anna Pavlova

The swans are blue ice now. They remember nothing
– Katya, Marenka who snapped bread
out of my palm with spoon-cold beaks,
their eyes keen as copper. Another hand,
old and yellow-skinned, a tax-collector's,
strains from the bank's shade. I swim closer.
It knocks, knocks at my chest. Only stage fright!
Naiads bring rouged cotton, little swans
fuss at my ankles. I shall run alight
in my own white pool towards the crowds,
and show all Russia the wingspan of my love.
Listen, the applause breaks like gunfire

as bruised roses spin through the smoky shine
to drop at my feet. Real birds die like this,
heavily, their broken wings ungathered.
Even the mooning swans, necks dipped to blue
mirrors, die like this. But I laboured
each night until I held another truth.
The bones of my shoulders melted into sighs,
my hands were little flames, their ripples perming
to pure air, my long feet curved
like the beaks of magic birds that never touched
land or lake. In dying there's no art!
When blood carved the snow in the palace courtyard,
I heard theatres weep. The old dance,
choreographed in thin bones, is fading
between these sheets. I rasp my last cries
to prove them right, young soldiers, real swans
whose wings flashed treachery, who fished in silence.

Going Home Time

Late winter noon,
the sky blue-black as taxis,
the street below
brimmed with fluorescence.
Typewriters stutter madly
as if they were trying
somehow to re-shape the sounds
for bread or anger.
My father stands
in the icy doorway
where a dim room meets
a darker hall.
His bent hands dangle,

useless even to smoke
a farewell cigarette.
He has only the threadbare
decision he stands up in,
and when they come for him,
no straitjackets, sedatives
or bribes will be required.
Easy as a child,
he'll tiptoe with the strangers
to their white car.
Fled into this city,
this cradling honeycomb
where all the girls shine
and shirt-cuffs are clean,
I know that I have simply
followed him here;
that this could have been his chair.
He stands at my side,
rubbing the ache from his hands,
amused by his child's
new game – the full in-tray,
the memos, the poems –
and saying with his smile:
no hurry, no hurry.
We all have to go home.

December Walk

i.m. W. A. Lumley

I

He can go outside, said the nurse,
and so I eased him
towards the door, and into

the last of the afternoon.
He was like frozen washing,
the arm my hand clutched
a brittle stick
from the garden's silvered blackness,
his complexion, white as a china-doll's,
and a pitiful, aged innocence
in his thin smiling.
The dark suit that wasn't his
hung on him.
The faded shirt, buttoned high,
had a crease ironed into it
where the tie should have been.
Clutching a shred of tissue,
he groped the few yards
around the hospital block
as if it were stony miles.
I tried to match his tread.
Perhaps he was right
and this was a great journey.
Perhaps a lifetime of hopes
and conclusions was arrayed
along that gravel strip
edging a muddy lawn,
and nothing else was required,
no afterwards.
I kissed him goodbye.
He shut his eyes.
Outside the day was still, breath-white
– the shroud he would be sewn in.

2
Pacing behind him,
I imagine how light he must be.
The bearers' tall, black shoulders

would never admit it.
They are braced for immensity.
The organ takes up the pretence,
and the chrysanthemums, trembling
their frilly gold Baroque
through icy chapel air.
In plain pews built
too narrow for kneeling
we remove our gloves
and pray from small books.
He was somebody once,
but sickened, and lost
all the weight of himself.
He forgot our names
and wandered for years,
words melting off his back
like snowflakes. I recall
barely a mood, a flickering
of smiled irony,
now as the altar screen
slides on its hidden runner
to blot out doomed wood
discreetly: that,
and a willingness, flat and English
as the whited winter sky,
to be always disappointed.
He was an unbeliever
in everything he did.
He would have had a hand
in this, perhaps, approving
our boredom, the sad weather
and what there is of ash.

A Marriage

Mondays, he trails burr-like fragments
of the weekend to London
– a bag of soft, yellow apples from his trees
– a sense of being loved and laundered.

He shows me a picture of marriage
as a whole, small civilisation,
its cities, rosewood and broadloom,
its religion, the love of children

whose anger it survived
long ago, and who now return like lambs,
disarmed, adoring.
His wife sits by the window,

one hand planting tapestry daisies.
She smiles as he offers her the perfect apple.
On its polished, scented skin
falls a Renaissance gilding.

These two have kept their places,
trusting the old rules
of decorous counterpoint.
Now their lives are rich with echoes.

Later, she'll carry a boxful
of apples to school. Her six-year-olds
will weigh, then eat, them, thrilling
to a flavour sharp as tears.

I listen while he tells me about her sewing,
as if I were the square of dull cloth
and his voice the leaping needle
chasing its tail in a dazzle of wonderment.

He places an apple in my hand;

then, for a moment, I must become his child.
To look at him as a woman
would turn me cold with shame.

Double Bed

She goes upstairs early,
lies wretched in the double bed,
letting its cool space ease her.
The curtains strain a thin daylight.
People move faintly beneath.

Tired out, she enters soon
those inner vastnesses
where wishes are almost naked,
pursuing new shapes
of desire, new solitudes.

She wakes fractiously
as the bed rearranges its sinews
for a heavier transport.
He brings her cold flesh
and delicate flattery:

and at length she plays her part,
breathless, half-drowning,
while he straddles her as if
he would life-save her.
He's not a brute;

she's not all innocence.
It's just that, by daylight,
they inhabit different angles,
no longer wave and smile
from each others' mirrors.

So, not unkindly,
he turns his back
(he can never sleep facing her)
and she will lie staring
at the dark for hours,

motionless, disarrayed
in the space he has left her.
It is too narrow to sleep in,
but impossible to leave,
she thinks, without robbing him.

The Skin Politic

Sails for the dark-blue trade-routes
Guns for the jungle
Mulberry-trees for Brick Lane
White skins for England.

Smiles for a passport
Pavements for wet walking
Ramadan for emptiness
White skins for England.

Airmail for memories
Shudders for dark nights
Swastikas for bus-shelters
White skins for England.

Long words for governments
Short words for street corners
Last rites for promises
White skins for England.

A Latin Primer

for Kelsey

Today, a new slave,
you must fetch and carry, obeying
plump nouns, obstreperous verbs
whose endings vacillate
like the moods of tyrants.
Say nothing. Do as you're told.
Dominus servum regnat.

Tomorrow, a legionnaire,
they'll have you building roads.
Clause by clause, you'll sweat
to span counties, withstand armies.
Pack the stones tight and straight.
Don't stop to pick flowers.
Milites progressi urbum ceperunt.

One day, you may discover
that even Rome was young.
And this is literature
– to hear your own heart-beat echo
in the bright streets of grammar
where poets lark and sigh,
and girls, like you, are choosy
– *Da mi basia mille, deinde centum,*
dein mille altera, dein secunda centum . . .

Gifts and Loans

They meet in the mornings over coffee,
their only bond, work, and being married
to other people. They begin with jokes

– the chairman, the weather, the awful journey –
delicately pacing out their common ground.

Later, they expand into description.
Families, who might not recognise themselves,
are called up in brisk bulletins,
edited for maximum entertainment.
(Gossip ignores their middle-aged laughter.)

She shows him a photo of her sons,
tanned and smiling over fishing-nets
one green June day when the light was perfect.
He talks about his daughters, both away
at college. They admire everything.

Through the months more curious, more honest,
they cultivate small permissions, remember
each other in the fading summer evenings,
and suddenly get up from their lives,
to hunt for a book, or pick some fruit.

No quarrels cloud the simple space between them.
They imagine how their adequate weekends
might shimmer with this other happiness
– and how, perhaps, they'd still end up with less
than haunts a gift of pears, a borrowed book.

The Strawberry Mark

Every Sunday, we'd set out at noon
and wear down the light to a dust of stars

before turning home. Our child went with us,
billowing the green sail of my smock.

Do you remember the farmer who disturbed us
on the shady edge of his corn? We ran like fire.

Monday would put us in our different places.
You worked, I queued, dragging the heavy basket.

The strawberries plumped as their price went down.
I ate them, craved you only.

Our walks got colder and shorter.
The house reintroduced us, two strangers.

Come November, I would find
the hem of the green smock suddenly drenched dark.

Alone, I walked and walked the edge of the world,
my breath the great wind there. You thought me lost.

Someone said: 'It's a girl!' You lifted the shawl
and saw the scarlet dappling on her thigh.

Twelve summers, and thousands of strawberries
later, the mark has vanished,

the peculiar heat and fragrance of that summer
sealed, perhaps, in her smile. Or simply faded.

Disco on the 'Queen of Denmark'

The North Sea drags our keel from noon to noon,
And, when she kicks, we who have trawled the moon,
And pinned those dead, glass oceans to our maps,
Tumble below to flay with Scotch and Schnapps
The old god, Fear. An oil-rig, dressed to kill
In lights, our messianic money-mill,
Stands starboard, crying 'Blessed is the Pound!'
And in the flickering Disco, to the sound-
Track from *Jaws*, elaborately we prey.
Our streamered hair glows pink, as surf makes way
For civilisation with its fizzing measure

Of music, sex and hope, its will to pleasure
Edged like a stylus, bravely swinging north
Between the winter stars, the berg's white tooth.

Days and Nights

It's a summer day very nearly like any other.
The pollen count rises in the afternoon.
An Iranian child steals a lemon in Selfridges.
The discontent of the unions rumbles dully
like a pit disaster many miles away,
while, in a murmuring classroom,
a young teacher is telling her six-year-olds
about the miracle of the loaves and fishes.
The first Royal Garden Party is held,
and afterwards the small hills of Green Park
stream dark suits, pastel hats, flowing skirts
and the low, excited conversation
of church-goers after an unusual sermon.
Even the tired marquee waitresses,
leaving by the Electrician's Gate
with sprays of left-over rose-buds, feel uplifted.
Two nurses, one on nights,
one, days, swap their only pair of shoes.
Along Park Lane there are lights and dinners,
middle-aged lust and young nostalgias.
It's a summer night very nearly like any other.
The traffic thins, the stars keep their distance.
The Chancellor dreams vaguely about the bank-rate.

Rules for Beginners

They said: 'Honour thy father and thy mother.
Don't spend every evening at the Disco.
Listen to your teachers, take an O level
or two. Of course, one day you'll have children.
We've tried our best to make everything nice.
Now it's up to you to be an adult!'

She went to all the 'X' films like an adult.
Sometimes she hung around the Mecca Disco.
Most of the boys she met were dead O level,
smoking and swearing, really great big children.
She had a lot of hassle with her mother;
it was always her clothes or her friends that weren't nice.

At school some of the teachers were quite nice,
but most of them thought they were minding children.
'Now Susan,' they would say, 'You're nearly adult
– behave like one!' The snobs taking O level
never had fun, never went to the Disco;
they did their homework during 'Listen with Mother'.

She said: 'I'd hate to end up like my mother,
but there's this lovely bloke down at the Disco
who makes me feel a lot more like an adult.
He murmured – 'When I look at you, it's nice
all over! Can't you cut that old O level
scene? Christ, I could give you twenty children!'

He had to marry her. There were three children
– all girls. Sometimes she took them to her mother
to get a break. She tried to keep them nice.
It was dull all day with kids, the only adult.
She wished they'd told you that, instead of O level.
Sometimes she dragged her husband to the Disco.

She got a part-time job at the Disco,
behind the bar; a neighbour had the children.
Now she knew all about being an adult
and honestly it wasn't very nice.
Her husband grumbled – 'Where's the dinner, mother?'
'I'm going down the night-school for an O level,

I am,' said mother. 'Have fun at the Disco,
kids! When you're an adult, life's all O level.
Stay clear of children, keep your figures nice!'

Consumerlit

This bookshop is being dreamed by somebody
who sits behind a desk and smokes cigars.
It expands shinily over several rooms and levels
– as dreams will.

These are enchanted forests
where crisp new climbers and sappy classics,
recently televised, are waving and singing
thoughts that are everyone's, simple as sterling.

And it is simple,
how the ideas fit their packages,
how the packages assemble the ideas
exactly as we've learned to like them.

The Market Wolf is dining on a new poet.
Literature is a colour-plate princess:
lightly she slumbers, waiting for your kiss,
in the shade of the Silmarillion Calendar.

Over the Bridge

Cowboys, free-rangers of the late-night bus routes,
they hit the town again, sucked cigarettes
fizzing as they lean into the edges
of corners, talk in nudges
and jeers – three ten-year-olds, too tough
for girls, though girls they'll brag of, soon enough,
their long, pale hair brokenly raked
beyond the line of last month's makeshift
barbering, frayed shirtcuffs falling short
to flash expensive watches, newly bought.

The city's greased and rapid
machinery is their passion; they'll work it
to the last cog, discovering all the loopholes
– how to tilt the pintables
and not lose the game, when to slip
their pocketful and saunter from the shop.
School can't detain them; they've cut the nets
of that soft playground. The lesson drifts
above their empty desks like a will read
solemnly to the disinherited.

Westminster Bridge veers up. They clatter down,
jump for its back, are straggling shadows, blown
and tiny as they run to see themselves
V-signing back from windows of black waves.
Further and further now from the controls,
they wander out of history, though its spires
rise in gold above them. The clock's proud face
makes no comment, shines on some other place.

Before these Wars

In the early days of marriage
my parents go swimming in an empty sea,
cold as an echo, but somehow *theirs*,
for all its restless size.

From the year 1980 I watch them
putting on the foamy lace.
The sun's gold oils slide from their young skin
and hair, as they surface

to fling each other handfuls
of confetti – iced tinsel
and tissue, miniature horseshoes
of silver, white poppy petals.

I search their laughter in vain:
no baby twinkles there,
nor has Hitler marched on Poland
beyond the cornflower waves

this print shows pewter.
But that the impossible happens
eventually, everyone knows . . .
And when they swim away

the unsettled water fills
with shuddery, dismantled weddings,
a cloud unfurled like an oak-tree,
time twisting as it burns.

The Girl in the Cathedral

for Andrew and Joanna

Daring to watch over Martyrs and Archbishops
Stretched in their full-length slumbers, sharp-nosed Deans,
Princes and Knights still dressed for wars as dim
As bronze, slim feet at rest upon the flanks
Of long-unwhistled hounds; daring the chills
And dusts that cling to stiffly soaring branches,
This small eloquence is a stone so plain
It cannot go unread, a chiselled spray
Of drooping buds, a name, a date, an age.
Susannah Starr died at ten years old,
And no one knows why her timid presence
Should be commended here. While history filled
The log-books of these lives, she sat apart,
A well-bred child, perhaps, patient with tutors
And needlepoint, perhaps a foundling, saved
By some lean churchman, warming to his duty.
Quietly during 1804
The blind was drawn, the half-stitched sampler folded.
Whoever mourned her must have carried weight
And bought her this pale space to ease his grief
As if such sainted company could speed
Her journeying soul, or because he guessed
The power of one short name and 'ten years old'
To strip the clothes from all these emperors,
And rouse her simple ghost, our pointless tears.

Pleasure Island, Marble Arch

Time and tarmac have ditched the last
Creaking ghost of Tyburn. A car-swathed island,
Wooded and sown with fine turf, is the navel
Of this oil-fed, pleasure-rich half mile,
Its jewel, a square grey lake, restless as silk
Under the wind. Dull, now, with November,
It wears the haunted, half-resentful look
Of an off-season resort, waiting for life
To be cheap and bright again, a gift of strangers.
Then the fountains will leap like marathon dancers
Pushing white-muscled shoulders and sparkling hair-dos
Hour after desperate hour into the blue,
And the grass lie kindled gold under the plashy
Coloratura of many languages.
Wilkommen, *bienvenue*, the faded placards
Shout to themselves in the subway corridors
And a girl will move shyly in front of the fountains,
Smooth back her hair and smile into the future,
To be peeled from its eye, a tiny Hockney
Of blue light, spray and the delicate boldness
Of flesh in a mild climate.
Meanwhile, the grass dims, the stone basins
Eat leaves. A gardener stoops to his heaped barrow.
The island is ours, though we possess it
Only at a distance, from office windows
Or the tops of circling buses. We approve
Its elegiac mood, its little image
Of transience. Whatever storms tug
Bigger seas to madness, we trust this water
To move within imaginable limits.
It is stamped on our days, part of the pattern,
An opaque poetry, revealing less
Our sense of failure than our certainty
Of what's provincial, gardened, small, enduring.

Sunday Tea in the Village

The hawthorn's out in all its bright-eyed pink;
the village pond blinks up
through willow-hair, a focal point for bold
lovers and their cassettes.
Across the road, the downs, ploughed gold
by the late sun, could lead to higher things,
but here a painted sign
says TEAS, and it is time, we think, to stop.

We file into a church-shaped wooden shed
beneath St Mary's tower
(four-square and Saxon, comfortable as psalms
and litanies once were).
We ought to be shy Brownies or the Choir
– bona fide villagers. Instead
we're peering Londoners who've travelled miles
in faded jeans and sentimental smiles.

The trestle is a dream;
home-made preserves are lumpy jewels, small cakes
lopsided in their frills
like choristers who long to misbehave.
Some of the buns are shiny, some are matt;
some wear a touch of brave
scarlet, a swirl of cream
like decorations on a Sunday hat.

The scattered tables glimmer
with such crisp white, and brilliant, tiny flowers,
we think of scented trousseaus, by and by
snipped into baby things, then handkerchiefs;
the patient-fingered women
sitting at summer windows that contain
a postcard-sized St Mary's, trembling leaves
and huge blue sky.

That blue looks at us now,
huddled in jars, this year's forget-me-nots
already fading, hardening into seed.
Outside, long shadows fall across the gleam;
the evening sit-coms bloom,
rainbowed invisibly on aerial stalks.
And yet the past will not relax its hold.
It seems to faintly smile, waiting for us
like grownups for a child
who's run too far ahead, and surely, soon,
will stare round in dismay, and hurry back.

Almost in Walking Distance

Two centuries ago they would have taken
this same short cut through the farm,
the rough, scrubbed boys and girls to whom
corn-fields were work-a-day. In tight best boots
for the Sabbath, laughing tumbled country vowels,
on mornings blue and full of bells as this one,
they would have skirted the plait-haired rows
all the way to the crumbly lanes of Chaldon
and the parish church, their star,
cradled in a cluster of bent yews.

What's altered in the scene
isn't just the split sack of pesticide, blowing
from a hedge, the tractor waiting on the hill,
or the bare sting of my legs against the stalks;
it is my aimless pleasure in the walk
and the edge of melancholy it lends the bells
calling me to a hope I cannot enter
across fields I knew well, yet do not know.

Coming Home

The bar is full of English cigarette smoke
and English voices, getting louder
– a language lumpy as a ploughed field.
It's hard to believe our tongues have got it too.

People are growing drunk at the thought of home.
The sea patiently knits its wide grey sleeve.
No one else comes up to lean on the rail
where, damp and silent, we watch

the long white skirts of land drifting
sadly through mist, as if a young girl sat
by the shore still, waiting for a bluebird.
It's September, and already winter.

And now the toy-sized train
is creeping with its worn-out battery
and a cargo of sandwiches and arguments
over grey-green fields into grey-white suburbs.

We're playing a game with the streets
– spreading them out and tying them up again;
when they've caught us, we're home.
The lawn swells like a tiny English Channel.

We chug towards our own front door
anxiously, seeing as if for the first time
how tight the plot that locks us in,
how small our parts, how unchosen.

Star Whisper

for Eugene Dubnov

If you dare breathe out in Verkhoyansk
You get the sound of life turning to frost
As if it were an untuned radio,
  A storm of dust.

It's what the stars confess when all is silence
– Not to the telescopes, but to the snow.
It hangs upon the trees like silver berries
  – Iced human dew.

Imagine how the throat gets thick with it,
How many *versts* there are until the spring,
How close the blood is, just behind the lips
  And tongue, to freezing.

Here, you can breathe a hundred times a minute,
And from the temperate air still fail to draw
Conclusions about whether you're alive
  – If so, what for.

A Humorist in Spring

to Jerszy, at the time of the Falklands War

The grey storm-troopers of the wind pour into your rebuilt
 city.
They flush out litter from corners, they beat shirts and make
 whips of headscarves.

They try to knock down the neo-pasteboard government
　　buildings,
And tear the trees and fountains from the replanted squares.
You do not admire the cold heroism of resistance, its lack of
　　humour.
You do not admire the cold megalomania of the state, its
　　lack of humour.
You return to a country where the trees sway scarcely left
　　and scarcely right.
Their shoulders shake with soft green laughter. You are
　　shocked
to read in the papers how fierce and humourless our ships
　　are,
how the young faces inside them are packed like dried fish.
They slice into the sea as the tanks flow into your squares:
these great engines, some say, are the work that makes
　　freedom.

Writing the City

Rhymes, like two different hands joining,
are those slightly archaic correspondences
I look for when in trouble. It's so easy
to start panicking in cities.

All roads lead to each other, sharing slick
anecdotes of combustion. They sell
tin lollipops, barren islands
and the one-way look for city faces.

Things happen and unhappen; cars, like eyelids,
blink time away. I'm due for demolition . . .
That's why I stand so long in the Poetry Section,
and buy apples just to slice them into cradles.

The Carpet Sweeper

Mother, last week I met
that old Ewbank we had
when I was three or four,
standing outside a junk-shop
in Bridge Street. I was sure
it was the one because
it knew me straight away.
At first, we were both glad.
We looked each other over.
I think it felt the sharp
impulse of my pity;
it made no comment, however,
and I was too polite
to mention its homeless state.
Mother, the wooden case
was burnished still, and stout.
Its wheels were scooter-sized,
and, just as in the old days,
slyly it urged my feet
aboard to jiggle a ride.
I drew myself up a little
(I'd borrowed your scolding face)
and it apologised.
Ashamed, I turned to other
subjects, praised its lion
trademark, proud though worn;
spoke of the rubber mouldings
that had saved the shins of our chairs
when savagery and housework
boiled in your heart. Mother,
I'm sure it spoke your name.
The sighs of all women
whose days are shaped by rooms

played over it like shadows.
What could I do or say?
I turned, it became small
on the dusty pavement, trying
perhaps to recall the smell
of our floors, the cosy tying
of loose ends, scattered wishes
in its spinning brushes . . .

Double Exposure

for David Rumens

Come into my room now your better half
has floated off from you a little; don't
mock, don't make a noise, don't spill the coffee.
I'm playing house here, but it's tree-top frail,
so leave your gales and lightning at the door
and come and give me your blessings – what else
are the latest-model modern husbands for?

You can play too – why not become a student
again, and crash out on the sisal floor
of an obscure first-year Philosopher?
Show her some snaps – not of your holidays
or sister's cat, but the future, two giant babies
who come alive and roam about the room,
eating cake and groaning as you kiss her.
The bed looks comfy, but won't give you shelter.
You'll have to find a quieter afternoon
to marvel at the virgin you'll uncover
– double-exposed with baby-scrawls of silver.

Here, where our past and present planes bisect,
it seems quite natural, after dark, to find
the window holds a city and a room,

exchanging surfaces on blue-black film.
Look how the Post Office Tower wears my wardrobe!
A train hurrying out of Euston glides
its amber wishes through me every night
until I pinch the curtains close, decide
it's time for old techniques of black on white.

Above the single bed I've tacked a Klimt.
It's called 'Fulfilment'. If you'd noticed it,
you might have found it raised a few light questions.
A joke that leaves a bitter aftertaste?
A profound statement on the spiritual
rewards of celibacy? An adulterous comment
or just a wish, perhaps? You might have seen
more intersections than at Clapham Junction,
had you looked up and traced
that gilded dressing-gown with all its scrolls
converging on a decadent embrace.

'Time will say nothing but I told you so . . .
If I could tell you I would let you know.'
   – That Auden villanelle makes such a sadness
of infidelity, its echo seems
trapped in all single rooms where stalled desire
throbs like a light-bulb. So what *can* I tell you,
I, whose bed is chaste but whose mind loses
its grip with such poetic fluency,
you'd be quite justified in saying it cruises:

That freedom's not like being sent a cheque,
or working after midnight on a high,
or walking miles just for the hell of it?
That mine at least is brimmed with everything
we've ever had and held, and there's no turning
from our history? Since you arrived, these walls
haven't stopped flickering with its lantern-show,

and pictures of fulfilment flicker, die
and are reborn constantly in our eyes.

On a night that's Mediterranean-warm and dusty,
we drift to where the Space Invaders flash,
and street-wise reflexes are newly honed
by the imminent loss of ready cash.
The Camden of stripped pine and antique lights
in harebell shades has locked itself away
to dine. Greek music pours from windows dark
as wounds in scabby tenements marked 'For Sale'.
The plum-haired sons and daughters of tavernas
gesture like figures on an ancient frieze,
though words and clothes declare them Londoners.

I leave you video-gazing, leave you winning.
Small faces lift for kisses, nonchalant.
I'm clumsy at this weekend parenting,
but no one cries or argues. Back indoors
I add another bookshelf (just a brick
at each end and a plank across), and stack
the comics and Sunday papers that you've left
and that I'll never read – one more sad layer
of history. And then it's time for bed
earlier than I'd planned. (For in the dark
it's harder to see double, hard to see
at all, in fact.) A room's just floorboards, walls,
plaster, wood. And yet it's not the same
now you're not here to tell me where I am.

A Case of Deprivation

A shelf of books, a little meat
– How rich we felt, how deeply fed –
But these are not what children eat.

The registrar rose from his seat.
Confetti fell, and thus were wed
A shelf of books, a little meat.

We sang, for songs are cheap and sweet.
The state dropped by with crusts of bread
But these are not what children eat.

They came, demanding trick or treat.
We shut our eyes and served instead
A shelf of books, a little meat.

Then on our hearts the whole world beat,
And of our hopes the whole world said
But these are not what children eat.

Two shadows shiver on our street.
They have a roof, a fire, a bed,
A shelf of books, a little meat
— But these are not what children eat.

Lullaby for a First Child

This timid gift I nurse
as the one clear thing I can do.
I am new and history-less
as the name on your wrist, as you.
But flesh has stored a deep kindness
ready to welcome you.
Take it, a little silver
into your small purse.
There it will gather interest
— the warm, bright weight of you.

Skins

There are those that time will carelessly perfect:
Leather, wood and brick fall derelict
As if aware they charmed us as they slip;
This deal table, strung like a harp
With a silky glissando of dark grain
Blooms like a lover from the hands it's known.
Scrawlings of knife and bottle, child and guest
Have warmed its heart, a rough autumnal feast
Spilled into soil, becoming nutriment;
The wood's more deeply wood because of it.
But there are others, the most loved and rare
Time told them once of which the years despair,
Laughter has scribbled not itself but pain.
Each face is fallen on hard times of bone.
Money will court them first, and then deride them.
There are no masks but sorry stones to hide them.
Yet to the end they haunt disgusted mirrors,
As close as love, and steal with snow-lipped fingers
From little, lying, scented jars each night,
Skins that are pillow-shadows by first light.

Suicide Fantasy on Carfax Tower

The fivepenny bit wouldn't work the telescope.
It bobbed and swung hopelessly.

I was the captain of some failed spacecraft,
a black hole over one eye like a pirate.

How my silence hurt me
in this soft-stoned, many-leafed city,

so talkative and holy,
even the four o'clock bell

with more to say than I
on the important topic of dying.

Like targets in a video
war-game, the tiny shoppers jerked below

. . . But I was no Kamikaze:
I would time my obscurity

not to kill, but to astonish;
aim for the shifting

dot of the pavement,
not even brush anyone's coat.

How coldly and fluently
the swift air would disown me

but what wild running and ringing
would greet the stones springing

into brain-flowers of white and scarlet
like a medieval manuscript.

March, Happy Valley

Days that are finely stretched and luminous
as the paper of a Chinese lantern, keep
the birds up late and whispering across
the valley, where a massive wind feigns sleep.
All down the heath-side, dangerously close
as heart-beats to a foot that wades deep grass,
hang violets in the strangeness of their blue.
Luggageless, perennially new,
with ancient heads that they can only bend,
they have arrived more quietly than the dew
to feel the perfect cold of where they stand.
The country has a used, dishonest face,

a look of sour back-streets where trade has died
though half the windows still pretend with lace.
Spring, the sweet spring, is a refugee child
grown old before his time, a hope displaced.

Museum

Pro bono publico,
bright wood, clear labels;
a tasteful history
of sand and fossils,

motto-bearing plates
and, along one wall,
like the Apocalypse,
'The Coal Coast' in oils.

Out on the real quay,
dogs are walked, the flat
water takes a slice
of sun from the smokeless sky.

The schools line up to go,
but the men in caps
linger shadowily
over toy-town mines, dolls' ships.

They get the place by heart
like the last day at the pit
or the drawer in the kitchen
where the strainer's kept.

Quadrangular

How to unfold the forbidden, scholarly gardens
was a trick I learned today
beside you. I practise it
alone, and a flat wall blossoms
perspective; a lawn,
stone backdrop and domesticated sky,
as astounding as if some tiny
sun-peeled door had disclosed
a casual stretch of marble,
a single fountain twirling
her white taffeta for no one.

To be in the garden at last
is to feel almost faint
with relief, like the right-sized Alice.
The lines drawn between
two classes that smile at each other
only through magic boxes
chained to the edges of rooms
dissolve in the merry lattice of our fingers.
While tourists are lectured, we
show each other round.
We'd like the walls to guess
which of us was never young here
— as if they didn't know.
I think they're scared by our mingling
of awe and disrespect
like some lost art of rhetoric,
the tight little problem we set them
by the plus-sign between us.

Afterwards, the light
blooms soft and yellow, forgiving.
On stones ripply-haired

as Pre-Raphaelites, our feet
dutifully part,
and only the page is left.
Here is the miniature plot
where I've laid fresh turves and paving,
opened a quad of words
with solemn, churchy shadows
for you to wave across.

Cherchez L'Ail

London that night was held by golden ropes
    Fraying through the river's black.
The 'Queen of Spain' with all her costly lives
Sat tight, as we sat, formal in our hopes,
The bottle on its ice-bed leaning back.
We touched the cloth with bright, impatient knives.

Tides turn, the damaged love-boat drifts away;
    The marriage-teasers walk
The plank, and one in torment almost screams,
But smiles instead. I sniffed my hands next day
To light those flames that stroked our ice-chink talk,
To meet you on the garlic breath of dreams.

Siren

Your children are your innocence, you prize them
greedily, three pink fingers dipped in honey.
At night, three souls slide in their perfect skins
into a rippling length of light. You bend,
damp-curled, still marvelling at the little bud
of abandonment, each tiny, cracked omphalos,
how it is almost an opening that you

might slip into, ticklish, precipitous,
a hair's breadth widening from tenderness
to pain. Sleeked as if by recent birth,
hair cleaves to each small skull, neat as your hand
to well-soaped limbs. So your relinquish power
to babble and disport with the loopy tongues
of child-talk. You have three faces now
with three clean smiles for the mother goddess.
I stand apart, waving a small goodbye,
and noticing that my innocence too has drifted
off with your limpid fleet, just out of reach,
leaving me pure sex, a dangerous pulsing,
a light that sings and warns on the bare ledge of self.

The Hebrew Class

Dark night of the year, the clinging ice
a blue pavement-Dresden,
smoking still, and in lands more deeply frozen,
the savage thaw of tanks:

but in the Hebrew class it is warm as childhood.
It is Cheder and Sunday School.
It is the golden honey of approval,
the slow, grainy tear saved for the bread

of a child newly broken
on the barbs of his Aleph-Bet,
to show him that knowledge is sweet
– and obedience, by the same token.

So we taste power and pleasing,
and the white wand of chalk lisps on the board,
milky as our first words.
We try to shine for our leader.

How almost perfectly human
this little circle of bright heads bowed before
the declaration of grammatical law.
Who could divide our nation

of study? Not even God!
We are blank pages hungry for the pen.
We are ploughed fields, soft and ripe for planting.
What music rises and falls as we softly read.

Oh smiling children, oh dangerously gifted ones,
take care that you learn to ask why,
for the room you are in is also history.
Consider your sweet compliance

in the light of that day when the book
is torn from your hand;
when, to answer correctly the teacher's command,
you must speak for this ice, this dark.

A Christmas Carol for Heroes Old and New

'Since this/Both the year's, and the day's, deep midnight is.'
JOHN DONNE *A Nocturnal Upon St Lucy's Day, Being the Shortest Day*

It's the year's midnight (I won't count how many
Since your last candle shivered out); now only
        Scholars try names
On the lost She who aped attentiveness,
And clasped your hand, its clever helplessness,
        To Poetry's reins.

So you ride out their noise, and history's,
Across the pyromaniac centuries
        To these bright streets.

Hot-line and waveband mesh the stars above;
Down here, the snow grows sluttish at the shove
        Of booted feet.

As for the fact it's Christmas, there's no doubt
In London; neon and tinsel spell it out
        Wherever you're turning,
And though the sun was sepulchred all day
There's a warm flush in the four o'clock night-sky
        Of money burning.

Recruited to our throng, with a lean smile
You press your nose to these alchemical
        Gold-brimming panes,
And deftly lift from each department store
A pocketful of shiny metaphor
        For deepening pain.

Dear ghost, dissolving inkwards, reinstate
The mourning tongue, the negatives we hate;
        Show hollow plenty
Your whiplash lines whose very commas bite
Until the tears that smart like crimson, light
        Our frozen city

— A grammar for all those who move less freely
Than snow before the wind, or darkness stealing
        Across the floor;
For hungry queues whose meat and bread are doubt,
Closing ranks as the angle from 'sold out'
        Grows more severe.

The law in armour stalks their public squares
And rust-thin words are hammered to new powers
        On anvils of dissent.
At home, and tight, we chant a milder verse
To 'Peace on earth' (from Harrods to St Paul's)
        — Fine sentiment —

Though not conceded by the governing will.
The West stages its cold-war vaudeville.
    And it's as though
We'd purposefully forgotten being schooled
That here our rulers rarely shoot the ruled
    For saying no.

Between our market-place of wind-up stars
And the gross state with its new breed of tsars
    What's there to choose
But this hair's-breadth infinity where you speak
And utter your peculiar heart-break
    Part fact, part ruse?

So Art counsels the self, and rarely fires
A Lucy dead in conscience or desire;
    Yet tyrants fear
That poets are the thin ice of their times,
Their stanzas tiny casements where red crimes
    Brazenly peer.

Be Patron then, upon this darkest day
Of every fierce refusal to betray
    In words or silence.
Bless, if you've power, the art of all that's not
– Exile, and death, and freedoms re-begot
    From nothingness.

An Easter Garland

I

The flowers did not seem to unfurl from slow bulbs.
They were suddenly there,
shivering swimmers on the edge of a gala
– nude whites and yellows shocking the raw air.

They'd switched themselves on like streetlamps
waking at dawn, feeling wrong,
to blaze nervously all day at the chalky sky.
Are they masks, the frills on bruised babies?
I can't believe in them,
as I can't believe in the spruces and lawns and bricks
they publicise, the misted light of front lounges
twinned all the way down the road,
twinned like their occupants, little weather-house people
who hide inside and do now show their tears
– the moisture that drives one sadly to a doorway.

2

My father explained the workings of the weather-house
as if he seriously loved such things,
told me why Grandpa kept a blackening tress
of seaweed in the hall.
He was an expert on atmosphere,
having known a weight of dampness
– the fog in a sick brother's lungs
where he lost his childhood; later, the soft squalls
of marriage and the wordier silences.

In the atmosphere of the fire
that took him back to bone
and beyond bone, he smiled.
The cellophaned flowers outside
went a slower way, their sweat
dappling the linings of their glassy hoods.

3

My orphaned grass
is standing on tip-toe to look for you.
Your last gift to a work-shy daughter
was to play out and regather
the slow thread of your breath

behind the rattling blades,
crossing always to darker green,
till the lawn was a well-washed quilt
drying, the palest on the line,
and you rested over the handlebars
like a schoolboy, freewheeling
through your decades of green-scented, blue,
suburban English twilights.

4

In the lonely garden of the page,
something has happened to your silence.
The stone cloud has rolled off.
You make yourself known
as innocently abrupt
as the flared wings of the almond,
cherry, magnolia;
and I, though stupid with regret,
would not be far wrong
if I took you for the gardener.

The Emigrée

There was once a country . . . I left it as a child
but my memory of it is sunlight-clear
for it seems I never saw it in that November
which, I am told, comes to the mildest city.
The worst news I receive of it cannot break
my original view, the bright, filled paperweight.
It may be at war, it may be sick with tyrants,
but I am branded by an impression of sunlight.

The white streets of that city, the graceful slopes
glow even clearer as time rolls its tanks
and the frontiers rise between us, close like waves.

That child's vocabulary I carried here
like a hollow doll, opens and spills a whole grammar.
Soon I shall have every coloured molecule of it.
It may by now be a lie, banned by the state
but I can't get it off my tongue. It tastes of sunlight.

I have no passport, there's no way back at all
but my city comes to me in its own white plane.
It lies down in front of me, docile as paper;
I comb its hair and love its shining eyes.
My city takes me dancing through the city
of walls. They accuse me of absence, they circle me.
They accuse me of being dark in their free city.
My city hides behind me. They mutter death,
and my shadow falls as evidence of sunlight.

The Most Difficult Door

There is an ageing mirror by the stairs
And, next to that, the most difficult of doors.
This is where we live, the home's true heart.
Its furnishings, heaped for some moonlight flit,
Are combs and hats and scarves in slip-knots, all
embodying the female principle!

I sometimes think they must have swum like clouds,
My daughters, through those sea-blue altitudes
Of birth, where I was nothing but the dark
Muscle of time. I bear the water-mark
As proof, but that my flesh could be so filled
And concentrated, heart to heart with child

– It mystifies me now. I want to draw
One back, and this time feel a proper awe
For the tiny floater, thumb-sucking on its rope,

Slumbering in the roar of the mother-ship,
Or let my palm ride switchback on the billows
Kicked in my skin by silvery, unborn heels.

Instead, through thinnest glass I watch them drift
At leisure down their self-sufficient street;
Their territory might be the whole of time
Like that of lovers in some midnight game,
This house their port where indolently they sight
Far out at sea the changing play of light.

Sea restlessness! It haunts the oldest vessel
— A shanty murmuring under a torn sail
That no harbour is safe, nor should be safe.
Only deep waters lend full weight to life.
The maths of stars is learned by navigation,
And the home's sweetness by the salty ocean.

This glass could cut a vista down the years,
Gathering suburban satins and veneers
To a sleepy London bedroom. Hair, long-greyed,
Glows animal again; they touch, half scared,
In the spotless mirror, shining, crimped and pressed,
My grandparents, child-sized and wedding-dressed.

Now it is staring with an older face
— My own. The moon stares too, a steady blaze
of glass-flesh. Through these gaps we look at death
And turn our ways of cheating it to myth.
Nature wants children; we, her children, want
A fixed, more moon-like role, a monument.

We've watched the comb reap sparks from our live hair;
Now for the putting-on of mock despair
As timeless as these little pouts and twists
— A rite we go through as the cold glass mists.
We know the brightness in each painted eye
Must often be the brightness of goodbye.

My floating daughters, as I leave I'll see
How you will one day look as you leave me,
How touch draws back, malingering, though the breeze
Of night is tugging gently at our sleeves.
Be wary, but don't fear the darkening street.
I give you this, my opened map of flight.

Heart Sufferer

He stands in his kingdom of cloth, the long rolls
heaped in a stifling rococo all around him,
and smiles at the visitors' compliments. His eyes
are calm, however. He is no emperor now,
merely a guide. Business is a small thing
compared to a Bach fugue or even a prelude,
though balancing by day his lost currencies.

He speaks his adopted tongue with a fluent crafting.
except for a few cut vowels. But the poets he quotes
are all Hungarian, all untranslated.
He is recomposing a suite of piano music
remembered across the noise of thirty years,
this businessman who makes out an order so briskly
– three metres of small-check gingham in muted green.

His customers tonight are an English couple.
The man beats him occasionally at chess.
The woman he doesn't know. The cloth is a gift.
She presses it to her face, smelling the sweetness
of an orange giving its gold to the treacherous north.
He waits upon her choice, feeling December
creep from the walls, whisper up through his soles.

Here are satiny linings, cerulean
glints from the rarest birds, the earliest summers.
Here are the stripes of crops, a snow of flowers;

and now the flattened cities, tanks, collapsed
angles of aircraft; table-cloths once dappled
by the Sabbath candles, ravelling up in flame;
small bodies sewn into the colourless dresses.

He turns off the lights (no one else is allowed to,
he explains shyly – it's an old superstition)
and thinks of his tall sons, how they will never
wake the switches of his dying kingdom.
He climbs the stairs slowly, examining
the coats of his two visitors – brash young cloth,
not lasting. His heart warns him, beat by beat.

With luck, he'll leave its music at the door
of his favourite cellar bar. A dish of prawns
is light, easily swallowed. He breaks the necks
deftly, sucks the juice from each stalked head,
and wonders at his sin, the sea-clean flavour.
At pavement-level, London chains its gods
in light; he worships none, but wins each day
by his own kind of fasting and atonement,
time become paper-thin as the map of prawn shells.

Geography Lesson

Here we have the sea of children; here
A tiny piece of Europe with dark hair.
She's crying. I am sitting next to her.

Thirty yellow suns blobbed on cheap paper,
Thirty skies blue as a Smith's Salt-wrapper
Are fading in the darkness of this weeper.

She's Czechoslovakia. And all the desks
Are shaking now. The classroom window cracks
And melts. I've caught her sobs like chicken-pox.

Czechoslovakia, though I've never seen
Your cities, I have somehow touched your skin.
You're all the hurt geography I own.

A Cold Dawn

This is the sky that drank its bitter greenness
from the waters of Gdansk Bay.

This is the sky of the world, its forehead smeared
by the faded sacrifices of industry

and breath. This is the sky
that always shines into my room and makes a picture

of the moment of childish tears after a parting.
The first machinery creaks awake outside

like ice at a thaw. Blind hammers
grow intent on their fathering.

Soon, everyone's brain will be working,
shuttling the dark, slickened parts of an obsolete engine.

The Division of Reptiles slides
into the square, announcing its dialectic

to the ship-builder, hurrying
with lowered eyes over the bridge.

He thinks to himself, 'Blood fades.
These stains were wept only by rivets.'

So the snow-storm of light goes on
filling up the day,

and all the small *no's* are said
and lost in the monstrous *yes*.

from Regent's Park Crossings

Grand Designs

A perfumed handkerchief,
a bedspread of silk, a park.
His sun-sleeked horse carries him,

the seaside Prince,
away from affairs of state
at a glorious, graceful canter.

Taker of air and of slender
hands, he is the patron
of the three-hour lunch-hour.

In his memory, two glasses
kiss in a buried wine-bar.
He has left an art of dalliance,

its lovely formalities;
a path broad as four coaches,
a bank of encrimsoned silver,

drawn swords of fleur-de-lis,
ducks in fancy-dress,
footmen and maids abandoned in the grass.

Dark Path

Beneath this unlucky white May tree,
we found all we could understand of love.

So we went deeper and deeper down the green path
whose stems grow thickly together like a great friendship,

as if we were dreamed by some old nature-god,
and bound and garlanded with children's hands.

Darker and steeper the green path plunges still,
but now I've lost you; it's late.

Gnats play like little lights above the ghost crowds
of Queen Anne's lace, the lake seems made of dead rain.

What if all that has happened which we named
desire cries suddenly to be renamed?

Here come my two black swans, desultory.
They snap their beaks in the water and complain.

One always in tow to the other, through the seasons
they float their listless epithalamium.

Better, they'd say, an unadoring pair
than one in deep love, alone.

The Rain and Time

It was the rain, not time,
that drove us from our seat:
rain's fresh, abrupt and sweet

hilaritas, teasing us
with the bookish smell of dust,
the brightened traffic swishing

beyond that iron goodbye
– the gate – which suddenly
had become impassable.

We rushed from tree to tree,
caught not in time but the rain.
All night it stroked the dark,

and this was happiness
– not to care whom you held
while the flickering, whispering threads

held us. And somewhere still
on these dry, forgettable days,
perhaps it is stitched for us

dancingly, in minutes,
our life between-lives as it runs
caught both in time and the rain.

A Brooding of Mallards

The females are crowding the bank
with moody silences,
heads tucked in, wings crossed.

I turn to my imaginary companion.
'Perhaps,' I say, 'they have heard
that drought has been declared.

'Of course, it's men they blame,
swimming while the park burns,
their plump green cheeks like silk.'

He smiles. We walk on
to the formal gardens. There
in flower-light, two lovers

have grown together like espaliered rose-trees.
Slowly they turn to each other
and sink to the gold-haired verge

as if pulled by the weight
of all that they desire.
A nest of differences

is closed with one winged shadow.
I cannot turn to my imaginary friend;
I have made him disappear.

Civilisation

This is the made world.
The geraniums are so perfect
they could be plastic

— apart from the peppery scent,
pure red. The grass has been trimmed
to within an inch of its life.

The lake is a blue piano.
The roses are better fed
than most of India.

Here are some children, shrunken
in chairs offensively tall.
Manhandled, staked like dahlias,

and pushed towards the light,
they sit in on events of movement,
with watchful, tearless eyes.

The old nod their heads.
Their yellowish colours split
into calcified smiles, pure white.

Nothing

Your absent presence spoke
softly across the summer
with your haunting absence.

I was between the two,
a child whose timid look,
swinging from eye to eye,

is a metronome of dread,
knows nothing, nothing, nothing
but his guilt-ridden innocence.

So shifts this sea of grass
beneath the wind, until
the sun burns it to stillness

and gold. But what is kept?
The daylight turns its back,
slips the transfigured quilt.

Mediocracy

Nothing here is sad or complicated.
The Open Air Theatre will perform
the same three comedies again this year.

The dolphin-boy is a legendary confection,
the drinking fountain, a folly.
The Bandmaster sticks to the light classics,

his shiny regiment buzzing around Sousa,
as if Schoenberg, after all,
had chosen a sensible trade.

Et in Arcadia ice-cream
and billowing deck-chairs.
Each grassy lap is nurtured by the state gardeners,

and picknicked on by the masses.
It's an English Utopian's dream
where the laws (against walking

on certain banks, and fishing
the duckponds) are so pointless,
everybody obeys them.

A quiet, shared happiness bathes
like a sunset, each limited choice,
and only the very few

are tortured by mediocrity.
They are, of course, free to leave
at once by the Golden Gates.

Tulips

The tulips parade for May Day
– Galata, Golden Niphetos,

Rosy Wings, Abu Hassan
– all the glorious fighting units,

polished, drilled, not one
man short, happy as sunlight.

They glow like a great flag spread
over a nation's dead.

We admire them; we can't quite love them.
Their faces are hot and closed

as if they had seen torture.
At any moment, we know,

they could twirl in the dandified ballet
of the firing-squad, to face us.

And yet, it must be admitted,
they're a clean, well-balanced lot.

At night they sleep like the guns
of good fascists. Nobody plans

suicide, gets drunk,
falls in and out of desire.

Serene, they have finished with self.
No, we can't love them. But sometimes,

deep in our dreams, they call us
to name our freedom, and then

pepper us, not with bullets,
but with bright medallions of laughter.

Reckoning

At dusk, the park is suddenly occupied
by hungry lovers. Their hips swing together

dog-like along the dim paths.
The chestnut trees flick little white embryos

at their feet, their feet burn them brown.
Life is always on the verge of a massacre.

Look where the tulips have been pitched
headless, their rigid figures

starved and blade-like, red
smatterings of their flesh

stuck to the earth. Look where the daffodils leaned
to be photographed, each one

convinced it was the star.
They died as they were loved

— *en masse*, a whole generation
of perfectly creamed complexions

rubbished and outstripped
by nature's great law of green.

Now the sky glows the colour of lampshades
in a bistro, the trees are black

crowding big-shouldered like waiters,
priests, aunts, pall-bearers.

Our flustered, red-faced lovers
can't get beyond the *hors-d'oeuvres*. They dip their fingers,

while the chestnut-blossom ticks,
ticks with the sound of a pen-nib totting numbers.

Phaedrus

The souls of lovers, said Socrates
to his young companion,

can complete their wings only
by embracing Philosophy.

The way hard, these friends
paddled the stream, arousing

a bright complication of water.
Through the hot midday

their silvery dialectic
shimmered below plane-leaves.

Summer wings stirring the air,
love talked itself to oblivion.

They parted not with a kiss
but a prayer, honouring wisdom.

Evidence

A cold silk of dew over my feet,
a mask of smoke on the sky:
the evidence of an ending's scarcely in sight.

The leaves are still afloat
on their threads, and green as neon;
the flowers, feverish, tousled,

are proud of their high colour.
Yet all over the park,
pulses are being taken, anxious murmurs

gathering. Privacies, summer-deep,
are smashed by feet among leaves,
hands sliding under stalks.

Here is a shock of bare earth,
an empty bed; whatever
was lost has carried its name beyond recall.

Imagined colours dawn
and I catch sight of you,
your jaunty walk, proud head

tilted, showing your profile
brightly submissive to the sun's yellow pencil.
I touch you, but only death

with his dark smile and philandering embrace
turns in acknowledgement.
Still the evidence is slight;

the leaves float on their threads
green as neon, the flowers
lift their mouths for more light

(since even the sick must eat)
and on the lake, dressed
for a wedding that's a funeral too,

paired charcoal swans dip questioning
necks as fuzzy-soft as baby's hair,
their beaks the two cruel colours — flesh and blood.

Numen Non In Est

The city's ravishing make-up
is all over the sky
in teary streaks;

the sky is hurrying out.
The frightened flowers have sunk
their last coins into moonlight.

A runner heralds himself
with the gasps of crushed leaves.
The breath he unstintingly pours

is kept by the wraith trees;
now they're as lost as he is.
In the clearings are temples,

their pitch roofs low
as frowns. They are dedicated
only to shade.

All winter they'll stand empty
for the dark god has escaped;
his love is everywhere.

Fallen

The sky is leaning and leaning
towards the park, grey breast
suffusing the green with shadow.

The light is crushed between them.
They exchange slow breaths
in heart-to-heart dumbness.

I touch, deep in my pocket,
horse-chestnuts found for the children
and never given.

Dressed in their creamy caps,
they glistened like brushed colts,
silkenly sat in the grass

– creatures of the dew
and a moment's lending;
impossible, but I took them.

Now there's no need to look.
I can feel how the light has gone,
how the tree is dead in them.

They are museum pieces
– old conscience money, carved men
for a game of imagining.

Appearances

How like a branch a man
who stands in a high tree.

Blackly he bends on the bending
bough in the blind light.

Smoke rising towards him,
he patiently saws, diminishing

his own margins of safety.
He'd fall with his branch, of course,

in the next frame of the comic,
pursuing to its limit

this art of camouflage
now gathering its echoes

– a moorhen's weed-green legs
– the absurdly familiar smiles

of two who have just met
and share by chance their seat.

Pavane for the Lost Children

When you rest in my arms and your heart
quietens against mine
I think of a midnight kitchen,
the kettle muttering on the lowest gas,
and the baby forgetting to feed,
lips plumped like a little mollusc
that is almost losing its grip.
They could not relinquish survival,
those lips; I knew what they dreamed of
would keep arousing them
to fits of greedy, absent-minded tugging.
So I sat on, enthralled,
and inexhaustible
as the fated wedding-jars.
This too is our grown-up devotion
when fatigue is most pressing:
to pretend we will never put each other down
and drift singly away
on sleep's disappointing persuasions —
such lowly forms of life, so deeply marine,
we cannot move apart, or know what time is,
but are turned like bivalves on the lifting wave
that has promised us to the sand.

Time Trouble

I know all about these German wrist-watches.
They try to wake you with tinny, insect-like tunes
by Kapellmeister Beethoven,
as the digits flip over on your bedside table
and my old-fashioned minute-hand
flies to your neck and whispers nervously
with that little pad of fat where your head is thrown back
because you're still in an ecstasy of sleep,
and your suitcase not yet packed.

Once upon a time
they'd take me to admire the German clock
in the museum. There were wooden figures inside it:
Jesus at wooden supper
with his twelve wooden apostles.
And when it struck three, they said,
the apostles filed out
and all bowed woodenly to Jesus
except Judas, who swung round the wrong way.

I never stayed to see this remarkable dumb-show.
By a minute to three, I was going to be sick;
I turned my back on the clock, the crowd
fell apart with a hiss.
As I race down the shadowless aisles,
though the horrible whirring has not yet begun,
I can see it all perfectly
– mad Jesus, his nodding guests,
and Judas, the simple materialist,
turning on his clockwork,
showing us his chalk-white face.

Circe

Now we are nothing. It is as you wished
when we last held each other.
I saw you boyish, crass, forgivable
and mythic with departure
– but it was something that you'd come at all.
Surely your presence underwrote return
and surely all the brightness in your eyes
belied the casual phrase
by which you cut adrift our misty future.

Oh yes, I had your warm life by the neck,
yet somehow washed you in oblivion
like Lethe, for you went from my bed
that afternoon forgetting everything.
What is between us now? No conversation
or kindness – merely waves
that roll pig-grey, rinsing the silent cables.
Each night I try and drink my way across
– a moth-like weaving
to find the chancy formula, the voice.
Sometimes I drag it to the telephone.
My finger slips, I've been too long alone.
I could do an aria or a speech
perhaps, but how make small-talk of so much?

I think of you in sunlight
your body dark, local drugs on your lips,
god of the vines, banal as an advert
but for the greedy shining in your gaze.
It falls upon Penelope, betrayed
that afternoon, so unimportantly;
you take her now because she's there, and simple,
unspoilt as the little cove you've found.
She has no song but offers you her mouth.

You give her all your kisses,
nicknames, money, whims (she loves you child-like
among the brilliant in the best hotels).

The breeze at sun-fall flares
suddenly and shakes your salt-stuck hair.
The fig-trees start their soft, accustomed screaming.
Our northern dusk is slower,
a schmaltzy, dim, blue church for sick abeyance,
with love and pleasure always somewhere else
– Eden, Jerusalem, Arcadia.
The sirens can be moral – if you care.
Remember me, my faithful touch, my shape
before I aged, became entirely graceless,
all envy, all desire, all lack of hope,
condemned to sail upon a self-wept sea
each year-long night, Odysseus, of your absence.

Vocation

Is it poetry I'm after at those moments when
I must clothe your hands in mine, comfort your shoulders
(so bare and neglected sometimes when we wake)
or press your mouth to taste its uncurling flower?
Is that which seems so fleshly and truthful merely
a twisted track into words, a way to leave you
for your image? Art is tempting, a colourful
infidelity with the self, and doubly feigning
when what is repossessed secretly by one,
was made by two. If poetry were only vodka,
we could gulp it from twin glasses unanimously
('I poison myself for your health' the appropriate toast)
– or you, a graphomaniac, you might warm
to my heavy-petting dactyls, the squeak and creak

from locked suburban stanzas . . . as it is,
my tapping fingers are lonely. They perceive
how they have clung to moral adolescence.
Their vocation now could be simply to talk to your skin,
to take you at kissing time: later, to close your eyes
by stroking the lashes lightly over cheek-bones
flushed with some high, bright, childish fever, and so
write the poem in the touch-shapes of darkness,
and let it end there . . . They are on the tip of trusting
this silent, greyish room, its astonishing view
fading from metaphor to the life with you.

Revolutionary Women

Nechayev, dreaming of Tsar-death,
wrote about three kinds of women,
and how they could be harnessed to the cause.
The first he dismissed as painted, empty.
You could use them, twist them, toss them away.
The second were good comrades, passionate
idealists, willing workers,
but dangerous finally, and disappointing.
Their values weren't political at all.
They too must be discarded, or reformed.
The third type were the true revolutionaries,
deft with gun-oil, bullets, high explosive.
They'd take a lover only for his secrets,
milk him fast, and leave him in his blood.

I know I'm with the second sort, cherishing
nothing better than a just cause,
except perhaps the man who'd die for it;
who watches in a daze allegiance melt
like candles at the hovering hour of bed-time,
to rise again in reconstructed gothic.

Turning soup into a bowl, I've gasped
at a white face in the china, both yours,
Nechayev, and that of any bourgeois,
gazing up in naked appetite.
This is what causes the strong hand to falter.
Armies, official and unofficial, know
that what they kill aren't men, or are merely men.
But we, that regiment of the starry-eyed
you need and fear and try to educate,
who type your manifestoes through the night,
may still in the morning be discovered,
the counter-revolution breathing gently
beside us on the pillow, while the Tsar
goes to breakfast, and his men to torture.
In our loose nightgowns warm and obvious,
too slippery to cement a single brick
of the just state, even the state of marriage
– Nechayev, you'd be right to gun us down.

In the Cloud of Unknowing

Goodbye, bright creature.
I would have had you
somewhere on solid earth,
wings clipped to pale

shoulderblades,
and your fleecy head
a chrysanthemum, darkly
grown from my pillow.

I would have kept my tongue
for what salt weepings
it could tease from your finest
silences.

But it was written
into your book of life
that I should be brief.
Forbidden to count

the ways, denied
et cetera,
I worshipped the stone
from your supper-time plum,

the little hairs gleaned
in tears from the sheet.
Metaphysical desire
was all they would bear,

a bandage of art
for the low sob
of the vernacular,
a condition of prayer.

Now when I wake
and the dawn light names
your perfect absence,
I am at home,

lapped again
in my earliest language,
the vocatives gilded
with desire and distance:

'Thou who art called
the Paraclete';
'After this our exile';
'O Sacred Heart!'

Dear iconoclast
forgive these texts
their cloudy haloes.
The intent pen burns

its slow path through
the slant rain of Greek,
the stars of Hebrew
. . . to touch your hem?

No, it was never
possible.
The old mystics knew
as they closed the book

on the dancing colours,
worn out with words
never made flesh
and with flesh that fought

their long abstraction.
They listened a moment;
the breath-soft footstep
in the cloisters faded

as always to sighs;
the cold congress of leaves
in darkening autumn;
the wind's dissolution.

Northern Woods

Small enterprises line the exit roads
out of London . . . then the bankruptcies . . .
and the long haunting of her absence begins
in a delirium whitened by birch-trees.
They sidle past, existentialist poseurs,
with a soft slippery shine that is barely a shine
– what light is there in the world for them to borrow?
Go on, they say, dissolve into drugs and tears;
we are her trees, we are your memories

blank with all she could not bear to tell you.
But I never cry. I just keep driving, staring.
When I left her for the last time, our hopes
the sea-smashed continent, my flight-bag heavy
as a new tongue, I learned to swallow fire.
Now the colourless bottle leaves me sober
as a vision of birch-woods, growing colder
and cloudier as they get to Pietarsaari.

A Jewish Cemetery

1

At dawn they are one shadow, whispering.
They are warning their children:
don't break the backs of your books.
Sunset. The shadow multiplies;
the backs break.

2

Among the swaying sighs
and the candlestubs, gothic with catarrh,
wanders the upright citizen. He is bored
and uneasy. He shoves the broken bits
of alphabet with his boot.
What else, these days, can you do with the past?

3

The closed books.
East looks West and sees East.
West looks East and sees West.
But the apocalypse rides both ways.

4

Names must often be silences

in this city, in this world.
His block of flats is dark
and hollow like a chimney.
I climb it twice a day,
doubling my heart-beat
as I touch the bell that bears
his faded, biblical name.
My hope spirals up
and falls back, levelling
with my lack of hope,
a conversation of kinds
between the flame and the ash,
between the name and its silence
in this city, in this world.

Winter

So it begins
with mist, a dazed bee
in the lavender-bushes
and radiators mild
as human skin.
This would be May
to your serious habitat,
the iron-black river
that is its heart-line,
wobbly as a frontier,
untrammelling itself
in endless dissatisfaction.
I think of the *Burlaki**
trussed in rope
like performing bears,

* The men who towed, on foot, the barges of the Volga River.

who trudged the plashing weight
of their servitude
to the rhythm of the thaw.
You bow your head,
fists on the table,
chest-notes swelling,
and silence the room
with their empire of grievance.
In your perilous climate
the wind has already fastened
stiff white grave-clothes
on the auburn water.
It settles everything
like the hand of a lover.
So the winter river
accepts its birthright
calmly, as you must
– the massive silences,
the gift of utter cold –
locked in its own
solid crystal, surveyed
by a few tethered craft
hungry for a new trade
of skins and revolution.

Aubade

Light as a rose
he sleeps beside
his first cradle,

intent on stillness
but breathing firmly
as if breath would always

give itself back.
He has travelled far
to be in his flesh,

to learn what happens
and to forget.
His existential

smile is perfect.
It tells me how
he will offer himself

when the time comes.
But for now he will keep
his excellent secrets

— the glossy function
of heart and lungs,
arms and legs,

the legend of his mouth.
His voice sleeps,
his sex sleeps.

In the faint shine
of morning, when
flesh can be chilled

I draw up the sheet
and cover him
to save us both.

Outside Osweicim

a poem for voices

1

Let me tell you the story of days, handsomely printed
in dawn and darkness, in sleep
and in burnt-eyed longing for sleep.

2

It puzzles the secular light, this polyphony
of dim cries. I wasn't there, I heard nothing,
yet the air is so full of them, I could sing them all.

3

When the train banged to a stop and whispered 'where?',
then they began. Some rose, some fell. The sky
rushed in like sea, we opened our mouths, it drank us.

4

It is hard to lose everything, harder to despair.
Those words on the gate, some dreamed of them, and loved
to walk in their shade, suck out the iron of their promise.

5

In the night, the bright light; in the wire, the stopped heart;
in the eye, fear; in the crust, hunger;
in the pustule, the flea; in the world, Osweicim.

6

Dumb narrative curiosity keeps you from the wire
how many times? You watch yourself, amazed,
whipped to a panting run past outstretched arms.

7

Death's clever, he has maths and capital,
but life's a tough nut, a phlegmy knot,
and nearly chokes him, like his Prussian collar.

8

They wanted us corpses and they wanted us
grave-diggers, they wanted us music, machines, textiles.
They kicked us as we fell. How human they were.

9

It was Erev Shabbat, evil was fallible.
A shaved girl smiled in the sun. An angel had murmured
'Amen' before he saw the gesturing dead.

10

And what if his Lord had heard that some of them
were raging animals, and still sent day-break, still
sent no one to stroke them with their names?

11

No, no, the question is obsolete.
Nothing sees nothing. Mercy was down to us.
Our mouths jammed shut on nothing.

12

Emblem, exhibit, witness – Husserl's suitcase
flanked the rust-brown pile. The cold twine of its handle
I touch, then grasp for a faceless, weightless stanza.

13

Child, enchanted at gun-point, whose child are you?
Come here, take off your cap, don't cry.
How is it possible I can make no difference?

14

Oh they crowd in, death's kindergarten. Small grazes
scared them once. Their eyes are always yours.
I'd take their pain, here, where your absence is.

15

I loved in you, yes, what made you strangest.
The desert gave you its shadows. I'd watch for ever
the poise of your smile, its bland, half-mocking stillness.

16

Another race is only another, strolling
on the far side of our skin, badged with his weather.
In love or hate we cast looks, hooks; get it wrong.

17

How shall I bear your indifference without hate?
It stirs in the dust, a length of hose. If I burn
how shall I not flex my whip near your eyes?

18

No, come away, put on that riddled cloth
of the centuries, be ash and stone, your stare
like his, a star.

19

They beckoned, they turned their limbs this way and that,
they whispered, you tried to get near enough to hear,
but the heat roared at you — take your eyes and run.

20

Not 'the six million', not 'the holocaust',
not words that mass-produce, but names. One name;
Husserl's, perhaps. His favourite food, his new watch.

21

Where death's made now, you must wear protective clo-
      thing.
Yes, we are still perfecting the science of last things.
Our blaze will be the best yet. Will you drink to it?

22

Chosen to illustrate the idiot's tale;
An illumination from the Book of Fire,
Sand and Next Year; chosen to be most mortal,

Our pyramid swam and sank through the nitrogen
Fog as starving crystals ate our air.
Christ, to whom the soldier said 'Go on,

Call down your god if he's got ears and brains,'
You would have understood our short-breathed terror.
Poor rebel son, you also wore our chains
In dumb commitment to the tribal error.

So we died for the last unforgeable scrap
— Ourselves. Got free for being something harder
Even than zoo-meat. Fought like the Crusader
To nail our resurrection to the map.

23

I died for nothing, no one. I was eighteen;
knew how to love, forgot; was beautiful,
then not. The train slides on across my shadow.

A Prague Dusk, August 21st 1983

About a subjugated plain,
Among its desperate and slain,
The Ogre stalks with hands on hips,
While drivel gushes from his lips.
W. H. AUDEN

I

When his broad shoulders turn
in their leaf-coloured uniform
and square up to a doorway
on Revolucni Street,
he might be any soldier
and the bar, any girl,
its response no more than a certain
heightened inattention.
He orders beer and seems
as innocent as his thirst,
straining his young white throat
to greet the last drop,
but the great, mellow, cultured
pearl of Mitteleuropa
has dimmed behind him;
shadows slide unchecked
from the medallioned buildings
scaffolded up to the waist,
numb veterans who have learned
how short the life of honour.
He smiles, provincial, brash,
half-tame. The careful hands
that have served his purposes
slink off and busy themselves
with rows of glasses, small
change. Eyes follow him out,

each glint of hate a coin
with its own private value.

2

That he could not master speech
no longer seems important.
Perhaps only a poet
word-trafficking in the free
market economy
of Oxford or New York
would have thought it a fatal weakness.
One blast of his breath was enough
to seal the twelve bridges.
With a few phrase-book phrases
he is armed for years to surprise
and entertain the natives,
his weight sunk deep in their silence.
Impassioned flattery
on the cut of his Westerner jeans
is not expected when,
naked as his fists,
he strides down Vaclavski Namesti
with his shuffling train of echoes:
what happens, happens without us.
We forget only the present.
It is the pall of memory
that sticks like morphine to the nerves
of the empty August city.

3

Going home on the metro
the children chatter
but the mother is almost asleep.
Some sweet, unscripted dream
is drifting across her face,

follows the droop of her arm
to the grasses that nod in her lap.
It's already dark
on the staircase where she hushes
and stumbles; light from outside
shines on the two pairs of shoes
placed at each nuptial doorway,
intimate and exhausted,
moored like little boats
in an ocean of drudgery.
When she too, at last,
is sitting in stockinged feet
and the children asleep,
she will recall each detail
of the picnic: how the country
they walked through never changed,
monotonous and tender
as the afternoons of motherhood;
how tall the grass became
when they lay down to rest
and the stalks rose silvery miles
and whispered to the sky.

Sappho

Alcaeus jewels her icon: – 'violet-haired,
holy, sweetly-smiling'. A later hand
– Ovid's – fires a heterosexual dart
as Phaon blunders from her lyric flame.
One little push, and she's a woman again,
the dark hair swirling at Leucadia's foot.

Surely she ground her bread on sharper stone,
entering history beneath some stained
old flag of power, Amazonian spark
spurting under the boot of the patriarch?
She glitters through the mesh dim Phaon trawls,
naming her girl-friends by an act of choice
as treacherous as talent; in its heat
are fused the stolen verbs: – to love, to write.

In a Room

In a room warm enough
for orchids, lit
apparently by candles,
a woman sits all day
considering her kingdom.

Valued as a princess,
she has always been taught
to brush out her hair, arrange
her ankles, and wait.
She is used to it all

– the sensation of hunger
– the need for patience.
She weaves her unplayed drama
from numberless muted hopes
and disappointments:

the sound of a car
stopping somewhere else;
a neighbour's phone ringing;
one letter on the mat.
Her heart barely moves.

Sighing, she turns towards
her mirror and witnesses
the familiar miracle,
flattered by artifice,
– real as its own pulse-rate.

She can cook and mend,
this woman, she can bear children,
dress a wound, translate
the abuse of the world into sweetness.
Among the mild machines

of her generous sciences,
untroubled by the clock,
unchecked, unspent, she knows
how terrible her power is,
how impossible not to use.

Waiting for the First Boat Train

An iron sky heats pinkly at its edge.
Chimneys are cold still, blue stones of dreams

in windows. It's as if we were at sea
already, floating on our platform-raft

out to the glinting swathe of rails, the dead
islands of sheds and padlocked offices.

One by one small figures dot the track,
their capes orange lamps, the small glow

of bed and kitchen slowly dampening
inside them as they file past our feet.

Daylight is waiting in its usual siding,
stacked in clean new metals. Their job

is to tap it down to rust and dark again,
building the years as signals click on silence.

Today, we are the light that floods their tunnel,
their moment of dazed forgetfulness,

bound for the sea, our schedules wide as hope,
our losses barely felt, like the weight of back-packs.

May 1976

That May when flowering chestnuts spilled not light
but words, black riddles printed on silk white,
in the green book of the park I read about
    a feast, a rout.

Two shadows wandered under towering trees.
Then one was gone. The other, in a blaze
of dread, lay down, perhaps it was in prayer
    to grass or air.

The names on streets, the names on playbills shone.
My bare arms earthed the sun. All that could burn
was you, in dreams more live than anything
    — my child, my ring.

The Advanced Set

My three mysterious uncles
were my father's elder brothers,
but not like him at all.

Arranged in steps, by age,
their three small portraits frowned
above the tea-time doilies.

They didn't frown at me,
but as if they sensed
each other's eyes, too close.

My grandma, sawing bread,
glanced back at them before telling
how they took care not to speak

when, by an oversight,
they were in the house together.
They ate in relays.

What did they do next?
They went to war. One
got taken prisoner.

(His tortured shadow lurked
dark-yellowish in the damp-stain
behind the print of Mount Fuji.)

One lived by the sea.
He had asthma and a mistress.
The other drank port-wine,

alone and grand in Tonbridge,
officer-class to the end.
Without a word they slipped

past my childhood gaze,

having never patted my head
or spun me a sixpence.

Those three Advanced Level uncles
— complex as love affairs,
far as the Burma Road —

might have talked to me in the end
but had the wit to die
before I grew tall enough

to sweep the brown photos down,
laugh at them, dance on them,
sigh, 'But you're ordinary.'

His Story

Just before the road curved to the sea
with detached houses packed and walled in flints
like knuckled hands, side-entries clean with sky,
there was a row of flat-faced cottages.
Each had unfurled the usual, neat, green apron,
hemmed with the usual flowers — except the last.
And here we'd always pause, my father and I,
to watch the waterfall. It ran quite slowly,
lipping its two blue bowls to fill a third
where fish sparked zig-zags round the dipped lines
of the fisher-dunces posed on either side.
We gazed. And then my father used to tell me
a man made this to please his sick daughter.
I always wondered why we never saw her.
This was our favourite route, we walked it daily;
the water gently flowed, the quick fish turned,
But no child ever came . . . Afraid to ask,
I thought that, Beth-like, she had been so good

she must have died. Thirty years later, why
in a dream did I see the garden, long-neglected,
grass hanging like drowned hair? Was there a man
who laboured at a gift that seemed ungiven?
Or was it you, my father, when you shaped
my thoughts out of your heart, before you took them
– your stories and my listening – into silence?

Denunciation

Maria Goretti was canonised
the year I started in Mother Columba's class.
The nun's eyes rolled saintwards
in her gnarled white face,
as she pictured the knife, its blade

nail-curved in an ivory claw.
We tensed. A peasant girl
and a labourer merged on the fray of the cornfield.
The sky blazed in the moment of the scream,
and the girl broke like a poppy.

By pony-and-trap she travelled
to the city hospital.
Blood ate through all her bandages.
'Imagine the agony!'
whispered the gnarled white face,

squeezing between our eyes.
How puzzling, how heroic
Maria Goretti's refusal!
She bled rivers for it,
died, and was made golden.

We drew breath again
on the journey north to Lourdes

and Bernadette, who coughed
in the little, unblessed stream
nipping icily over her sabots.

One day, through the playground fence,
I saw pale sky torn open
by a flame-haired Virgin. I sobbed,
but Mother Columba frowned like the Parish Priest
and washed her hands of me.

Greetings from Brighton

'One man's whelk may be another man's cornucopia'
JEREMY TREGLOWN

Now there's nothing
– only a mad, blue wall
building and toppling itself
hopelessly, over and over,
in the cage it can't understand.
We sit down abruptly like babies
and stare at our cuttlefish shins.
Everything ends here
– Victoria's wrought-iron reign
slithering like a chalk cliff
to post-punk Elizabethan;
the sound of flip-flops munching
the land's dish of leftovers;
the jeans and boxer shorts, melting
in a heat-haze of nudity;
London itself signs off
with a wavy flourish of neon.
We are locked in the mad, blue present,
an instamatic snap
from the eye of some child, a king.

His palace, a harem of curves,
billows behind us, his artists
are now perfecting the sky.
The other children have bought
a slice to send home, rock-bright.
They scan the polished crescent
of pointilliste sunbathers,
and readily pick themselves out,
so confident are they
that their particular gladness,
shadelessly gold and blue,
finds its true place in this.

The Inaccessible

At fifteen, I worshipped most of all
the inaccessible, their brilliance confirmed
by their continuing ignorance of my love.
The flux of growth, tilting me in its currents,
could not unhinge the skyline to which I pointed,
where dream and reality entwined their lights,
frail ariels flung across irreconcilable cities:
I touched down on my own imagination.
The streets were shrinking, but I didn't notice;
absence, the deserted square, shimmered beneath
fantasies richer than official roses.
How accessible the inaccessible seemed
with their moony apparitions, pauses, whispers
and yearnings tossed with love beyond wide screens
to meet a world of waiting eyes; my eyes.

Now tamed by gravity and sick of stars,
my body tensed for reports of impermanence,
my clutch of choices fixed as vertebrae,

fall in love a shade more carefully,
only to catch the hungry viruses
of what is possible, but lacks a root
in likelihood. I can no longer span
the irreconcilable cities, stroll unchallenged
across a mist of frontiers. In small rooms
under ordinary light, I hesitate
towards the not-quite-inaccessible
and watch them turn with whispers, pauses, gestures
forged from a private burning, crystalline
gifts for the eyes of other lives: not mine.

Letter from South London

Tonight I have no fixed abode, and write to you
sadly from the bus number 159,
where I brim my head like a child's sea-dipped bucket,
with swarmings of the city that I call mine.

The river's its usual brown, the sky dawn-misty:
across the jetty the summering crowd strays
lured by the pleasure-boats to a salt-free taste
of homelessness as the tideless water sways

between somewhere and nowhere, just like the state of mind
induced by sniffing rich diesel
and swinging round too many corners. Just now we passed
a souvenir-clock in the shape of a cathedral.

No time for that big, pale, V-signed face to calm us.
The slender candle-light of democracy
has flickered out in a gloom of broken doorways
where the winos study meths-economy.

Lives are still piled into flats, but the planners now
think lengthwise, thus decreasing

the incidence of suicide-by-leaping.
Tonight, it's almost Elizabethan how

the low balconies are encircling us with faces.
But they're already bored with watching us
languidly watching back from the stalled bus
— there's no reason why we couldn't change places.

This, after all, is metamorphosis country:
the dead cinema comes back as a Bingo Hall;
there's a Doner Kebab where Uncle's three satellites glowed;
nailed boards where the tears of Polish salami fell.

What does home mean? Money can smell of childhood;
work to the worker is his motherland.
It's an odd fact (though the jobless can believe it)
that the easiest way to belong is to be owned.

Nothing like that for us — no leases signed:
we occupied each other for a day,
and then took off, being children of the world.
Forgive me if, for a moment, I've lost my way:—

a compass-needle shivering sickly round,
finding no North to settle for; a tongue
paralysed by a language not its own;
a blood-stained shoe; a newly ringless hand.

Yes, though I'm local, that's the state I'm in,
while you, with your vivid Eastern darknesses,
seem rooted in our Saxon hypocrisies . . .
But, of course, you can't tell a sausage by its skin

(as the saying goes) and who cares where the pig was born?
A sense of belonging is something deep and private.
It flows with language, custom, habit — or
it can be aquired in twenty seconds flat.

So it was that I, transported carelessly,

woke to your smile and thought it must be home.
This, I agree, gives me no earthly claim;
simply means that there's nowhere else to be

right now. And it's not unbearable, all the while
I keep on moving. That's the city's fine
art of survival, freely recommended
everywhere from the ghetto to the thin blue line.

In Brixton now, to illustrate my point,
a dreadlocked boy comes racing down the street
that's his earliest memory (but Babylon, all the same),
and spills from his shoulder-bag a tape-cassette.

It clatters onto the pavement. The bus-queue shouts
'Oi!' (in Cockney). His eyes shine fear, but he lopes
back, picks up the cassette, and is off again,
all in a single, effortless round-trip.

He catches the bus, which roars like a ghetto-blaster,
reggae-ing down the dusty old A23
— a road joined, as the signpost reminds us, to Brighton
— though Streatham Hill has never seen the sea.

April in February

for Becky

At four, the afternoon's baby eye
is opened still – a miracle. The blue
fades slowly in my bare, west-facing window.
Its lingering is as sweet and new as April
– when folk still long to go on pilgrimages
through the old dust of houses, marriages –
your month. You wailed in that municipal
ward, in your pollen-coloured Babygro . . .

Birth tunes us sharp and makes us fall in love.
Then we must live with it. These days, you change
faster than the year, or seem unchanged,
depending on my light. Think of the downs
– still in their thick, rucked, winter pelt of mud:
small birds, circling on the air's lasso,
over and over each black, thorny crown,
find nothing creeping or unfurling there.
Yet if we walked towards them now, I believe
the hills would be all softly green and scattered
with those faint suns, those small, tremendous wishes
– the primroses of April, of your month.

Weeds

In gardens, it's the unwanted
babies that grow best and biggest,
swarming our beds of frail
legitimate darlings with roots
like wire and crude, bright flower-heads.

They seem oblivious
to the fury of steel prongs
earthquaking around them.
If they fall today, tomorrow
they'll stand all the greener.

Too soon, the beautiful lives
we've trembled over with sprays
of pesticide, friendly stakes,
and watering-cans at sunset,
give in, leaving us helpless.

The weeds, the unfavoured ones,
stare at us hungrily,

and since it is hard to live
empty of love, we try
to smile; we learn to forgive them.

Virgil for the Plebs

The child in front of the television set
bends half her mind to a dead language.

Its italics hook her down
between linenboard bent and scarred by generations.

Some progress has been made,
a teacher might say, reporting on the centuries

– a girl, and no patrician,
let loose among the big, imperial words;

yet, lacking the substance of self-love
we call class, tricked into myth

by special-offer potions for bright hair,
soft-focus studies in the art of kissing,

she's lost her heart for books,
says it's better to marry than learn.

The Trojans and Greeks were fighting over Helen.
Their ships and spears and shields

litter the page, stout but expendable.
Tanks nose across the screen.

Because the wars are in our living-rooms
we think them literature.

We can adjust them, strand the President
in silence, wipe off blood

in the twinkling of a switch.
Child-like we gather round for the old stories

of passionate nominatives and accusatives,
or, suddenly quiet, turn up the news to discover

the verb that waits for us
at the end of our sentence.

Two Women

Daily to a profession – paid thinking
and clean hands – she rises,
unquestioning. It's second nature now.
The hours, though they're all of daylight, suit her.
The desk, typewriter, carpets, pleasantries
are a kind of civilisation – built on money
of course, but money, now she sees, is human.
She has learned giving from a bright new chequebook,
intimacy from absence. Coming home
long after dark to the jugular torrent
of family life, she brings,
tucked in her bag, the simple, cool-skinned apples
of a father's loving objectivity.
That's half the story. There's another woman
who bears her name, a silent, background face
that's always flushed with work, or swallowed anger.
A true wife, she picks up scattered laundry
and sets the table with warmed plates to feed
the clean-handed woman. They've not met.
If they were made to touch, they'd burn each other.

Up Lines, Down Lines

I

A winter waiting-room where the gas-fire mutters
— Scarce tremor of blue filaments, scarce heat

Thinning towards benched walls — those benches hard
As the Ragged School — floor, walls and air one dense

Matting of nicotine, loud loose-boned doors.
Outside, a wisp of trees, a North Downs valley

Tarred for the greater work-force. It's a small
Drift of the casual or managerial

That settles here to an embattled leisure
Tented by *Telegraph*s and *Sun*s. The clock

Pursues its cautious policy of perfect
Accuracy twice a day. There's time

For the nine-thirteen to enter Merstham tunnel
At twenty past, time to get six across,

Or watch the vast statistics of collapse
Blur and devalue in a yawn. There's time.

A favourite cartoonist's simple moral,
A centre-page of packed bikini, hold

Dereliction at arm's length from the heart.
Cigar butts star the chill subsistence air.

2

Know that you'll see nothing beautiful on this journey,
But, swayed between a window and a book,

Let landscape hold you. Parse its rougher grammar
Of scrap-yards and sidings, house-fronts smirched

By their seven-decade dialogue with the railway.
Against patched, flap-skin windows, mouldering steps,

The sagging ropes of wet-bright washing argue
That lives are somehow made, and hold together

Inside, that crumbled plaster, spores of wet
Will dazzle to a symmetry of roses

Over beds where children lie. Read on towards
the common, and a man hunched on a seat,

Your train his book and window. Read the river
In slack-necked cranes like damaged birds, dank wharves,

Their last transactions closed. Study the tracks
Of slippery light that write your futue clear

Through the gathered shadows of the terminus.
It is your story. Enter with proud steps

Along a well-swept platform that last freedom
– To jostle at the gate. To take your wages.

3

Dodging their overseers – typewriters, Xeroxes,
Phones – those battering tongues of retribution,

From platform seventeen the year's first tourists
Chase flight down flickering rails. Beyond the station,

The airport; beyond grey sea, the world;
But the world is only a place of other stations

And other airports, doors that hoard no power
(though the sun silvers them) of greater worlds,

As they swing towards curved tracks, the flight-path home.
Cheated and tired on the same trajectory,

I wait, watching the smashed pane of a warehouse
Open a wound-black map the shape of Ireland.

Rain spits its beaded strings, skylights the rails.
We fly through hidden colonies, feel the breath

Of threats nail-packed and wired in attics, taste
Our own blood on the pitched-back stones of insult.

— These travel with us. But tonight we're hauled
Clear to safekeeping. Streamlets plait each gutter

As, hunched through the mild artillery of rain,
I run for a porchway, quickly step inside.

From Tonight's Programmes

He could say what justice is,
this prisoner, and the smashed teeth
in his frightened smile would serve
as sufficient metaphor
if only he wasn't unsure
of his right to words, if only
these lights, these difficult questions
weren't his torturers, starting once more.

This other, a prisoner too,
though relaxed in corduroys,
opening his book as the News
ends, and pain becomes art,
has a word for everything.
His vowels are ample, his heart
is good, as hearts go. He'd speak
the just poem. If only he knew.

Tides

The other night I slept in a red-roofed village
that was trying not to topple off the land.
Outside the Seamen's Mission a rusty-scaled
cod gasped for coins, standing tip-tailed,
but I turned in at the sign of the Dolphin, where
the landlord drank like a ghost at his own bar,
and his dog barked 'time' in the small hours.
I escaped at dawn to clear my head with the wind
that bounded out across the turfy clay
where at last the moor slipped into the arms of the bay.

Three hundred miles from the pinpoint of a chance
of meeting you, I was perfectly cool.
I watched the sea drag its malevolent, gleaming
tons away from the land it had just darkened,
and was glad I would be cosily south before
it hurtled back to boil at the sea-wall
and unveil a winter, the streets white or streaming,
the mouth of the mission-cod encrusted with ice,
and no one stooping on the pooly sand
to weigh the small cold of a starfish in a warm hand.

When I took the little creature from my pocket
later, I found it had changed shape, as if
in some last, inching retreat from life,
it had been reborn. I placed it in a glass,
freshly filled, with some salt from the breakfast table
– but it didn't stir again. I suppose I'd thought
it might unfurl like a Japanese water-flower,
brimmed with its element. So the foolish hope for
resurrection, or at least the kind of death
that brightens corn-rot to alcohol, driftwood to jet.

All that remained now was a valediction
to tender doubt, and the backward-racing lines

of the railway, sepia after a night of rain,
since I had to come home, leaving the dead starfish
for the landlady, leaving the village
to its history of cod and non-conformist virtue,
and the helpless plunge of its streets to their salty source,
leaving the chastened tourists clambering still
towards the mysteries of some clouded hill;
since I had to trade the rich North sea for stone;
talk with you, touch you, let the tide turn.

Waking

The house with its many windows drew the dawn
into itself, and light touched open shapes
and colours – a yellow quilt, our human darkness.
Pillow-grass flowered in all its varieties
– your lashes, soft as charrings, the crisp maze
curling along each forearm,
tiny needles of midnight in your jaw.
By the day's slow brightening,
I discovered the clairvoyance of your eyelids.
They flickered up, even before my lips
had found your sleeping face.
I loved your look of happiness, its pure welcome.
You touched me like your first-born, with a marvelling
sweetness that inventoried each part
and found me whole; yet you touched my heart
most when, climbing our tumult, you took its peak
with the candour of a child,
your quick-drawn breath half-cry, amazed by falling.

Lines

Remembering our lunch, alone and later,
what I get is a vision of a coat-sleeve,
black and creased, my own, complete with arm.
What was I doing, wasting so much time
    lost in the dark of myself,
    looking away from your face?

And that black sleeve swims before me like space
dotted with tiny stars of refracted light.
Your presence always had a curious grace
for disturbing the self-confidence of matter
    while dashing hope through the slip
    betwixt a cup and a lip.

Lost in that hour where flesh resurfaces,
we fed each other questions
– what we had done with the past, what we had kept
of each other, and lost;
    where we were now – the one
    that interested us most.

We were quick and brilliant cartographers,
penning our continent on the tiny scale
required for a plate to go from full to empty,
and a tablecloth to become the North Pole
    – bare, but for two glasses
    that might be our lost souls.

'Time's nothing,' you said, and as I smiled,
ready to doubt, I felt the furious slam
of lightning and its big immediate echo;
Suddenly I was in flames
    like a stripped tree.
    Your words were earthed in me.

How often, quivering between mind and gland,

imagination seems no more than the thread
from a child's hunger-wet mouth to his playful hand,
frail as the caterpillar's shaken guy-rope
    — yet this is what tugs and saves us
    as we climb; this is time's hope.

If, when we are distant points upon
an arctic blankness, tented and alone,
I can still drop you a line,
send it through dark, not fearing to be thrown
    on your mercy, this will be to live
    with stars sprinkling my sleeve.

And that delicate poise between what happens
and what's imagined will become our art
as long as we obey the simple lesson
of a meal and a wineglass, still assert
    the importance of common air
    to walkers on the moon.

Here is my rope-trick, then, requiring one
volunteer. Let's move towards each other,
not looking down, each word's taut centimetre
nearer the possible. Pursue these lines
    dear questioner, to the end
    and we will touch again.

Writing at Night

Light on the page, the shadow of a hand
slow as a carver's, leaving intricate trails
of cuts, the whiteness bleeding into black.
Notation of what we are, our heart-beats, hormones,
the chemical lights of the brain. The soft tick
of dotted i's, then the imitative rain

outside on claws. A little wind-animal
beats the back of the gas-fire where it's caught
in faint, metal shudders. The hand continues
over the page, gathering the massed night
which slowly reduces to a single line
joining our two rooms, our two lit selves
lost in the drama of their alphabets,
freeing the sentenced lives. I glance out at the dark,
and there's your face, written in shining drops.

Simple Poem

Why didn't the room say
how long your absence would be,
that night when you climbed the stairs
in your quick, expectant way
and sat across from me?
No word from the lamp or the chair
though they've both been around a bit
and ought to have guessed, not a sign
from the much-used willow plate.
It watched you laugh and eat
and did not seem to care,
as lost in desire as I
— and now you're not here.

And now you're not here, why
must there still be a room
with surfaces that mime
the slow life of the sky,
and a clock to strike off time?
Like an implacable heart
the blind swings open, shut,
on leafy blue, on grey.

Darkness refuses to stay,
and always the numb dawn light
shows a chair, raggedly turned,
and a small lamp that once burned
all through the summer night.
Oh how the light loved then
all the white length of your spine.
My pillow was dark with your hair.
Why doesn't everything die
now you're not here?

The Last Day of March

The elms are darkened by rain.
On the small, park-sized hills
Sigh the ruined daffodils
As if they shared my refrain
– That when I leave here, I lose
All reason to see you again.

What's finishing was so small,
I never mentioned it.
My time, like yours, was full,
And I would have blushed to admit
How shallow the rest could seem;
How so little could be all.

Advice on Interpretation

Notice the first theme is in the major:
simple, almost banal,
like happiness. Let it surprise you:
take it by surprise.

Imagine the beginning
of love, each searching phrase
preludial, delicate
as a fingertip learning a face.
Think of a smile curving
over deep silence, in the silence trust.
It should, of course, be played *cantabile*.

The first theme is developed
in a tumult of modulations
bringing back the second,
this time in the minor key.
Now every phrase must enact
the approximations of memory.
You are alone. Still
you shiver to the sense
of a fingertip, a breath,
and longings storm and break
across the bar-line. Listen!
It's as if time couldn't bear them.
And still, of course, you must sing, *cantabile*.

The Usual

It is a clear midsummer night:
They glow upon the cooling light,
The Traceys, Lisas, Janes and Dawns,
Barbaric and composed as swans,
For whom the world has yet to happen.
All day they've drowsed on close-clipped lawns,
Feeling their youth and colour deepen.

And now in chalky blue the moon
Melts like a tablet; lights go on;
In small front-rooms the power-packed boxes

Blaze into apocalypses,
Or storm the disillusioned street;
Plumped mini-skirts out-sex the maxis
– It's Sixties Night at Les Élites.

Life is the old deceiver who'll
Take every daughter off the pill.
They're after him in leaps and bounds;
He's got the stuff, he'll buy the rounds.
They laugh and jeer: – we know your kind!
But, after all, they like his pose;
Ravenous, thirsty, rightly blind,
They shrug: – what have we got to lose?

A Woman of a Certain Age

'This must have been my life
but I never lived it.'
– Her childishly wide stare
at some diminishing reel
of space and brightness, half
illusory, half not,
stuns to an epitaph.
And I can read it all:
how a little lie
whitened to twenty years;
how she was chosen by
something called happiness,
yet nothing, nothing was hers.
And now she has to turn
away, and her bruised eyes
are smiling in their nets:
'It's simple, isn't it?
Never say the yes

you don't mean, but the no
you always meant, say that,
even if it's too late,
even if it kills you.'

A Small Inequality

When a man loses desire
It's no joke
Either for himself or his partner.
Their mortification gives work
To the sober psychiatrist
Who may also enlist
The Marriage Guidance Counsellor
Or the Hypnotherapist:
Money will be no object.
All his house will cry woe
Till dreams or drugs re-erect
The master's libido.

But when a similar fate
Befalls a woman
It may simply amuse her mate.
Such 'moods' are common;
He cites the eternal
Headache and all
The 'no's' that really meant
'If you must.' And of course she still
Can please him if she tries.
This show will run and run
As long as he ignores (most can)
The glazed look in her eyes.

Academic Perks

Stumbling round Heathrow,
peering at hazy flight-times,
your handbaggage pitiless
with heavy reading
– including parts one and two
of *Serbo-Croat for Beginners* –
you're the perfect prototype
of the travelling intellectual.

That despicable English habit
of letting down the hair
in foreign climates
has never crossed your mind.

You cover your face
with your *Historical Guide*
when the plane unwisely begins
to get serious with the air.

'There are six republics.
There are five nations.
There are four languages.
There are three religions.
There are two alphabets.
There is only one desire: independence.'

At thirty thousand feet
what can you do but munch
half-frozen salami,
and silently repeat
such terrestrial certainties?

Shuddering, you touch down
not far from the workers' flats
and the new ring-road,

on whose wrong side
you will soon be travelling
towards the tallest hotel
in the many-windowed capital
(THERE, TO YOUR LEFT
THE FAMOUS SUGAR-BEET FACTORY
HEROICALLY OUTSTRIPPING
LAST MONTH'S PRODUCTION NORMS).

In your bedroom the first night,
trying to take in
the latest publication
of one of your learned colleagues,
that moon of a lamp-shade
drives you almost spare.
Its schmaltzy red glow
reminds you of a bar,
which in turn reminds you
how alone you are.

You pick the screws out
and watch it fall apart.

. . . But later, so much has happened,
your journal has turned pale
in the middle of Saturday,
and refuses to say any more.

And the last night you appear
to be a different person.
Somewhat dishevelled,
sporting the peasant-blouse
no peasant has worn
since the revolution,
you hum that famous
Serbian folk-song:
'*Let the lamp be as dim as it likes.*'

In the Craft Museum

Some nations lock up their poets. Ours have the key
to a high, clean room labelled Sensibility.

They have sat there now for a very long time,
and are clearly no threat to a democratic regime.

They are old, of course, but remarkably unspoiled;
their edges still cut, their moving parts are oiled.

Of course, they're permitted to go down to the street,
and the street may visit them, if it wipes its feet.

Here comes the guide now, telling the solemn young faces
that, yes, the poets still work, but don't touch the glass cases.

Ballad of the Morning After

Take back the festive midnight
Take back the sad-eyed dawn
Wind up that old work ethic
Oh let me be unborn.

After a night of travelling
How can it come to pass
That there's the same tongue in my mouth
The same face in my glass

Same light on the curtain
Same thirst in the cup
Same ridiculous notion
Of never getting up?

Cars stream above the city
The subway throbs below
Whirling a million faces
Like shapeless scraps of snow

And all these melting faces
Flying below and above
Think they are loved especially
Think they especially love

This is a free country
The jails are for the bad
The only British dissidents
Are either poor or mad.

I put my classless jeans on
Open my lockless door
I breathe the air of freedom
And know I'm mad and poor.

Love is the creed I grew by
Love is the liberal's drug
Not Agape but Eros
With his Utopian hug

And in the *close, supportive*
Environment of the bed,
He is liberty, equality,
Fraternity and bread.

That is the supposition
But I say love's a joke
A here-today-and-gone-tomorrow
Childish pinch-and-poke.

Perhaps I'll believe in something
Like God or Politics
I'd build those temples wider
But there are no more bricks.

Some women believe in Sisterhood
They've rowed the Master's ship
Across the lustful silver sea
On his last ego-trip

And some believe in Housework,
And a few believe in Men.
There's only one man that I want,
And I want him again and again.

He sat down at my table.
He finished all the wine.
'You're nothing, dear, to me,' he said,
But his body covered mine,

And stoked the fiery sickness
That's done me to a turn
– The fool that chose to marry
And also chose to burn.

Burning burning burning
I came to self-abuse,
Hoping I'd go blind, but no,
It wasn't any use.

I see a mother and her child
Both turn with starving face.
And that's the story of our lives,
The whole damned human race.

My conscience is a hangover,
My sex-life, chemistry;
My values are statistics,
My opinions, PMT.

Beside my rented window
I listen to the rain.
Yes, love's a ball of iron,
And time its short, sharp chain.

The middle-aged say life's too short.
The old and young say 'wrong'.
I'll tell you, if you don't like life,
It's every day too long.

Carpet-Weavers, Morocco

The children are at the loom of another world.
Their braids are oiled and black, their dresses bright.
Their assorted heights would make a melodious chime.

They watch their flickering knots like television.
As the garden of Islam grows, the bench will be raised.
Then they will lace the dark-rose veins of the tree-tops.

The carpet will travel in the merchant's truck.
It will be spread by the servants of the mosque.
Deep and soft, it will give when heaped with prayer.

The children are hard at work in the school of days.
From their fingers the colours of all-that-will-be fly
and freeze into the frame of all-that-was.

Split Screen

The gables squat like Dutch clock-cases,
    cosy and orange over Camden High Street.
A rabbi, gazing into the shoe-shop, stands
    between two baskets of left feet
– clean, unsmirched, made of some shiny substance
    God didn't make. Inside and out of reach
a better breed of foot tiptoes on glass.

Up the narrow stairs on Prinzengracht
    left, right, left, right the jackboots stormed.
The canal sunned itself. In Camden Town
    God's unconcern is not a talking-point.
The rabbi doesn't argue with himself.
    No one argues with him. Yet nothing's happened
to suggest old No-Name's had a change of heart
    since Anne Frank tried to live on Prinzengracht.

Some people kill, some die before they've lived.
    Shoes are the evidence of feet, but what
could be the evidence of perfect love?
    They've made a small museum on Prinzengracht
for the tourists to plod round. In Amsterdam,
    in Camden Town, you can buy a pair of shoes
or the Diary of Anne Frank. Left, right, left, right,
    the shoppers' feet stream by.

Passing a Statue of Our Lady in Derry

She appears tired, though dressed in fresh, white stone,
And bows the bandaged snowdrop of her head
Pleadingly to the bus – which hurries on
And leaves her stranded in my childhood,

Mother of small contritions, great hopes
And the lyric boredom of the rosary
When miracles seemed at our fingertips:
She is much younger now than formerly,

And in her narrow, girlish hands, she weighs
Not holiness, but a frail, human idea
That might accomplish anything – dismiss
An army – or, like childhood, disappear.

A Dream of South Africa

Trafalgar Square is only a pigeon-sea,
but he could hear the waves sigh up and fall
as he passed the sooty door-stones of Pall Mall.
The men in their navy suits were sailors, he
a brisk cadet. He marched behind, in step,
towards the lighted windows of his ship.

An office job! It didn't seem like work,
So I painted it in childish, Admiral colours.
My mother laughed, fought off the social climbers . . .
In fact, he was a ship-broker's clerk,
the fourth, last, disappointing son,
sea-feverish since the age of seventeen.

Cathay Pacific, Cunard, Peninsular House
– one night not long ago I followed him
– saw where he boozed – the Travellers', the Reform.
The wind hustled his stumpy, pin-striped ghost,
practised now, and as managerial,
almost, as if he'd been an admiral.

He stayed becalmed in these local pools,
drawn by the whisky siren's easy mood.
'South Africa,' she whispered, and he glowed,
imagining that palm-green, palm-court cruise,
a charming old imperialist of the fleet,
who'd crunch the diamonds under hard, white feet.

If he had doubts, he didn't ever say,
although he sometimes talked about retirement.
Once, he brought home from the Embassy
a pamphlet – boring, but it sounded decent.
It offered 'separate development for the Bantu'.
'Apartheid' tripped my tongue; a long word, new.

I've never understood what happened later.
My mother grumbled no directorship,
no retirement cruise, no Africa.
Age moves so fast, the young just can't keep up . . .
The liners that slid, shining, down the Thames
had sailed without him. Or he'd sailed without them.

Cathay Pacific, Cunard, Peninsular House:
I listed them, as he must have done

with boyish love, before he veered off-course
– wrong man, wrong job – but kept his head down,
having a wife and daughter to support,
until the lights went out on his horizon.

Ashqelon

At Ashqelon, I searched
a diaspora of sea-shells
for the perfect affinities
of size and patterning
that make a couple.

Little hinged bivalves,
they were unpartnered now.
Marked out for loneliness
as faces are,
each knew its sad uniqueness.

The sea had never valued
their delicate compacts.
It had plunged them into war,
then dragged them, fighting and broken,
and beaten them into the shore.

There they lay, one nation,
bathed in a flickering dream
which every sleeper read
from his own eyelids.
And, as I gazed at them,

it was as if the sea
scattered them still, or the wind,
and whirled their coloured rain
to the ends of Ashqelon,
and to shores that have no end.

A New Song

for Naim Attallah

'Thou feedest them with the bread of tears; and givest them
tears to drink in great measure.'
PSALM 90

Silences of old Europe
Not even the shofar
Can utter: Maidenek,
Mauthausen, Babi Yar

– Death of the innocent being
Our speciality
Let us add Lebanon's breaking
Sob to the litany.

So many now to mourn for,
Where can the psalmist start?
Only from where his home is,
And his untidy heart.

We pluck our first allegiance
With a curled baby-hand,
Peering between its fingers
To see our promised land;

Yours on a hillside, clouded
With olives; mine a cot
In a London postal district,
Its trees long spilled as soot.

The war was all but over:
It seems my new-born cry
Was somehow implicated
In yells of victory.

But it's the quieter voices
That keep on trying to rhyme,
Telling me almost nothing,
But filling me with shame:

– Germany in the thirties
And half my family tree
Bent to an SS microscope's
Mock genealogy.

Duly pronounced untainted
For his Aryan bride,
My uncle says it's proven
– There are no Jews on our side.

Ancient, unsummoned, shameless,
The burdens of prejudice:
All through my London childhood,
Adults with kindly eyes

Muttered the mild opinions
So innocently obscene
(Hitler was not 'all stupid',
and 'not all Jews are mean').

Later, the flickering movie;
Greyish, diaphanous
Horrors that stared and questioned:
Has God forgotten us?

Oh if our unborn children
Must go like us to flame,
Will you consent in silence,
Or gasp and burn with them?

It is so late in the century
And still the favourite beast

Whines in the concrete bunker
And still the trucks roll east

And east and east through whited
Snow-fields of the mind
Towards the dark encampment;
Still the Siberian wind

Blows across Prague and Warsaw,
The voices in our head
Baying for a scapegoat:
Historians gone mad;

Thugs on a street corner,
The righteous gentile who
Pins Lebanon like a yellow star
To the coat of every Jew.

Silences of old Europe
Be broken; let us seek
The judgement of the silenced,
And ask how they would speak.

Then let the street musician
Crouched in the cruel sun
Play for each passing, stateless
Child of Babylon,

Conciliatory harmonies
Against the human grain,
A slow psalm of two nations
Mourning a common pain

– Hebrew and Arabic mingling
Their single-rooted vine;
Olives and roses falling
To sweeten Palestine.

At Kibbutz Amiad

These are the solid texts
– houses in white lanes
scribbled with jacaranda.
But it's in the margins

we'll find our poems
said footloose Mandelstam.
I weigh this as you sleep
and all the kibbutzim

of the Upper Galilee
grow moody with children
escaping vaguely home,
tired as the khamsin.

Quarrels, piano practice
– nothing is lonelier
in this story of families
than our marginalia.

We keep ourselves to ourselves
in a flower-shadowed house
with an empty second bedroom
that cannot fathom us.

Camouflage

Hot Rhine-Valley days, the misty odours
of pollution and Late Romanticism;
hubris on a meagre city beach
where I am burning my base self to gold,
shifting with the sun as it slyly escapes
at an odd, foreign angle, never overhead,
thinking it something like our conversations
in the tongue we cannot share, haunting, oblique:

twilights that whirr with home-flying bicycles
and a perennial, anxious excitement
in case the night should betray its incredible promise
– for we are moody and unverifiable
chameleons of a thousand joys and troubles;
parted by so much daylight, we might arrive
at our violet-skied, electric meeting-place
as strangers who must touch each other's skin
over and over, and still not quite remember:

night, and the reading is from Dostoievsky.
Your new voice, fiery, rough, argumentative,
astounds the room, I dare not look at your face,
until at last the flare of language dies,
dies back to the dark garden
of breath and watching. Sunlight glares from my skin
like a confession, but my secrets are white.
You comment on my 'distinctive markings'
as I home towards you through the branching shadows,
fierce and intent, in perfect camouflage.

Eclipses

Midday. The earth holds its breath,
the shadows can't move an inch.
Only the sky seems to be rushing away.
It vanishes into the blue of its furthest blue,
dropping a little curled handful of sun-smeared iris
onto the world for us.
The poppies are clear glass bowls of some inky night-cap,
the grass, an amazement of light.
And you and I, what are we,
our soft, random collision
eclipsing us in this garden,

this room? Pass your hand
quickly over the sun's brow and invent
a glowing midday dusk
where I shall undress to my ear-studs
and you, to nothing. Where the exotic, slow,
brachiating animal we evolve,
time-lapsed, will have no name,
and I'll press my lips by mistake to my own skin.

Laboratory Visions

for Peter Meades

A suspiciously light, bright room,
it had surely been planned
for advanced psychological torture.
There were interrogation-cells,
where the subjects faced the wall,
rows of turntables
and slender miles of tape
packed around miniature cart-wheels
whose fast, fluttering spin
took my breath away – almost my fingers.
Dry-lipped, I sat down;
preparing a full confession,
ducked into the headset.
It fitted like a migraine,
the two black pockets
crackly as lightning.
When it spoke, I marvelled
– the voice was human.
I became human too.
Among the towering words,
I was a stranger, still
gripping with both hands

the luggage of my local grammar,
but getting acclimatised
simply by breathing the air.
And then the room I was in
was an ordinary kitchen,
cramped and high above Moscow.
Smiling uncertainly,
a woman turned from the stove.
She greeted me. I answered.
Zdrasvutye. Kak vas zavut?
Hello. What is your name?
For a moment our languages were mirrors,
and I thought I was in heaven.

Wire Baskets

Real-fruit yoghurts whose nutritional benefits
are said to be vast, but which will be spooned with a fearful
delectation that never exceeds half a carton;
baked beans with their modified starch, sugar, water,
cheerful as Belisha beacons, civilising
the most unrefined slice of toast; stout, country burgers
70% pure beef; bright young Grannies
from police-states, gleaming as our teeth should gleam,
gleaming as if waxed by the ardent housewife
I never was: – these I remember. I believed
I was structuring my children's bones like crystal
palaces, cheaply but strongly and beautifully,
just as the state, which offered free education
in those days, was fitting out their immortal minds.
My own was a supermarket of clichés, e.g.
every child has an inborn right to vitamins
and scholarship, whatever the parents' net income
. . . It isn't true of course. They have no rights

which the law can't take away and we had no right
to conceive them in such innocence, rosily tumbling
like shabby storks out of the sixties sunset
into the broken-classroomed eighties, beaks
and wings ripped off by the weight of our wire baskets.

West Berlin Eclogue

Hans's country retreat
was a few minutes drive from Head Office,
but country, nevertheless.

If we weren't quite at ease,
neither was our taciturn host,
born on that side of the Wall

where nobody would splash graffiti
to make themselves immortal.
There were too many tongues, adrift

and tipsy with cross-currents,
for one simple picnic;
but the grass befriended us,

and the thick gooseberry hedge
that marked the boundary
between the woods, birch-misted,

and our luminous clearing, dropped
its sweets into our palms.
Someone began 'Kalinka',

and Hans joined in, loudly
word-perfect, commandeering
the drama of its tempo *rubato*.

The sweat broke on his brow
like raw grain; we could tell
his success was superfluous

to the sinews of the Komsomol.
When the small fire-roses
had faded in the charcoal,

and the flats and sandy shallows
of a mildly remarkable sunset
flooded darkly over,

he lit the hurricane lamps
ranged along the privy roof,
and ordered us to dance.

Then, with a slight sigh,
he sat back watching us,
his feet in their triple-striped

yellow Adidas jumping
on the overturned beer-crate
like two insane bees.

We were babbling nightingales now,
paired and cradled and brilliant
with impromptu history.

Drunk, we knew every language,
and that every language was touch,
every wall, a gooseberry bush.

Incident in Pushkin Square

A refusenik is handing out leaflets.
After a minute or two,
the militia turn up and arrest him.
They study his literature
deeply for several weeks.

It is passed under microscopes,
tested for radiation
and chemical substances.
After much thought and conferring,
the authorities have to admit
that page after page is blank:
the refusenik has said nothing.
Nevertheless, he is tried
and found guilty of subversion.
He gets fifteen years' hard labour.
Silence, after all,
is a message easily read.

Seroyeshky

We broke slim boughs to stir
and sift the leaf-mould.

I was befogged by earth-colours,
my earth-bound sight an Axminster

of swirling oakleaves, beech-mast,
till I had trimmed my focus

to detail, even acquired
a touch of your magical foresight.

Seroyeshky, you called them:
mushrooms for eating raw,

but better cooked, you said,
in spite of the nickname.

Some were pale red, some amber;
the slugs had frilled their edges

and nipped small coins from them:
still, they were beautiful,

thrusting up stoutly,
bursting the thatch of their caves,

and yet most breakable,
their spore-weight slight as grass.

The Pinner woods were glowing
in a Muscovite sunset

as we brought home our catch.
You cleaned them and fried them

to a milky gloss;
eagerly we dipped our forks.

The bitterness was astounding.
We've been warned, I said.

Whatever else they look like,
whatever they are, elsewhere,

here, they are toadstools,
here, our enemies.

And so we abandoned them
– our prized seroyeshky, love-sick

fantasies of tasting
the past, or another's country.

The Compass Plant

Ya skuchayu pa tebye

'I am bored without you'
is Russian for 'I miss you',
but somehow weightier:
east of the Brandenburg Gate,

boredom can be very black.
It gets a whole mouthful of sounds
with a cruel twist at the end
like something Fate might do.

It resembles 'escutcheon'
– a bat-like museum-piece,
solid, medieval, filthy
with a coat-of-arms we can't read,

declaring the thickness of blood.
Bored as a sentry, I've taken
to vodka and dictionaries.
I guzzle words like a fly-trap,

but am really a compass plant,
my leaves tracking the sun
with blades perpendicular
to the incoming light,

irreversibly orientated
to you, your tongue, your absence.
If I seem to be asleep,
my senses are open wide;

I am highly photoperceptive,
and geared to the trembliest rumour.
All future-tense, I dream
bored into borders, opened.

Lovers in Westgate Gardens

When I passed them, tucked away
On a bench cut deep into the privet,

I observed two masculine hands at urgent play
On a small, cotton-clad, feminine ribcage,

Which seemed content to lie there and accept
The attention, snug and close as a bird in its plumage.

At once your absence swept me, fiery-cold,
And common envy, spiteful, mean and dull,

Froze to my skin. I thought how, when we loved,
I could do something better than lie still.

Then a sharp rustling shook the dark-leafed bower;
The lovers faded, you sat quietly waiting

For me to notice you, to sense you'd spoken.
'In love, the one pleased has no less power

Than the one who pleases. To accept with grace
Is also to give.' And then, it seemed, you opened

Your arms towards me so consentingly,
I was enfolded in that mystery.

Second Lives

Wedging himself by degrees
through the unlatched door,
the foundling tom cat

with his double set of neuroses
looks at the woman in bed,
decides he needn't leave.

They listen to the plug
knuckling the wall's far side,
then the granular buzz

of coffee-beans spinning

into fragments of themselves,
truer than themselves.

Around her stand the dead,
risen as usual,
encumberings of teak

veneer, uncut moquette,
thin brass and sprigged plastic
glooming in the dawn

of her second life.
The man who left that crumpled
space on her right,

chose them carefully.
She knows in which junk-shops
and at what price.

He was by himself,
breathing in the strong essence
of private owernship,

tongue-tied and stateless
as the tense face that dodged him
from mirror to speckled mirror.

This is his second country;
she, his lost wives;
she is twenty, thirty, forty

as she waits for him to bring
the Oxfam tray
with its dusty wicker plait

and scribble of poppies.
He'll set it gently down
on the quilt's collapsing flesh,

and, stepping back to watch
her childish pleasure, taste
the day's first sip with her.

Dark Harvest

They shine like tiny apples, black,
exhaling gin and loneliness:
the easiest fruit of all to pick,
but firm against my tongue's duress.
So I interrogate their skin
kindly, tactfully, knowing that soon
they'll have to break, confess their lies
of ripeness till my own mouth cries.

A bush of fruit-lamps burns as clear
in Harrow as in Chistopol.
It brings the life you fled so near
I'm dizzy with its taste and smell.
I wade breast-deep, the whispering bush
opening up against my wish
those glints and lights I least can bear
— the darkest eyes, the softest hair.

They have survived their altered state,
your exiled loves. They stir their tea
with little clouds of summer fruit,
and test the sweetness patiently.
Your absence falls as light as dust,
now, on their lives. They're almost used
to swallowing what's dull and cruel.
I think they almost wish you well.

Winter Borscht

Don't look for spies or angels in our kitchen;
We're Christmassing far from all religions.
Utopia doesn't mean a thing to us,
And we've forgotten how to talk with children.

Eating, though, continues. And ever since
I dipped my spoon into this wavy, scarlet
Winter sun, lifted its cap of beet-leaves,
I've felt as festive as a wedding-taxi

Climbing in clouds of exhaust and frost and ribbons,
With a bride who'll simply giggle and take snaps.
(The sandy, pointed beard, implacably growthless
Under its arc-light, needn't expect a visit.)

Then, of course, back to the revolution,
The uneatable sundae casting turd-like shadows,
And not enough spoons, and too many elbows.
Finding myself in such an official portrait

I think about God again, and the *chutzpah* of those
(Christians) who made their text-book so alive,
You could hear the jostle of wings, the musical pings
Of the haloes all the way from Florence to Kiev.

They too loved red. In fact, their rosy seraphs
Were here before us, bowed towards our plates.
Look, they've left us both a faint, indelible,
Golden sign, a blood-stained halo-print.

Love Poem

I said: When you leave our bed in the morning
at your unearthly hour, cover me, please,
with the quilt, because my arms without you freeze.

When he rose at six, I kept my eyes shut.
I thought: He'll remember, but he may not.
My shoulders were losing heat, but I kept my eyes shut.

I heard him gather his things and go out.
I fell asleep and dreamed,
and I was thinking, even in the dream:

He was in a hurry, it doesn't mean
he doesn't love me, no, of course not.
But when I woke up I was under the quilt.

Icons, Waves

The scalding gulp that almost clears the glass,
love rushes to the human eye, and lends it
illusions of a focus so exact,
a driver might lurch out, steer straight to death.
But we, late diners who've got tired of dining
and turned to iconography, believe
inaccuracy is also revelation.
Under the broad lamp with its singing bulb,
we stare into each other's brightest stares,
unselfed with curiosity, archaic,
and paint each other in a universe
where nothing's lost by lying in perspective:
I have the details — red formica table,
rinsed baked bean tin with its clutch of spoons,
your flatmate's skinny plant, the sallow glitter
of our once quickly filled and emptied glasses.

*

It was a dangerous ship we put to sea in,
over-freighted, dressed in Baltic ice,
crewed by the breath-clouds that had been your story.

Burning hope like kerosene, it suffered
the magnets of exile, every wave.
And though we raised our glasses, splashed our beer
with the sly diminutive brewed for thirty degrees
of ideology and new-year frost,
our toast was the vanished harbour of Atlantis.
I'd come aboard for word-trade, narrative,
warm money in my hand. You silenced me,
and it was then I felt the monster turn
his armoured intricacies under the waves,
and follow us like whispers, like ice.

                    *

So we'll be ageless, therefore timeless; so
we'll leave our heavy, fascinating shadows
on the doorstep; so, I said, we'll simply trace
in unobtrusive strokes what we are now.
You cracked the mystery fish, peeled the caul
from the red crayon of roe – which you gave me.
What part of taste, what part of time is this?
The bathrobe keeps slipping from my shoulders,
but we've been married silver years and gold
– a bare breast would neither shock nor rouse you.
Tell me their names – this fish, this salty planet
so like and unlike earth, its bright omphalos
a kitchen table. Minutes ago we were strangers,
hours before that, lovers. It's two o'clock
I said in the new language; that's nothing, you said,
your mouth full of scales, that's children's time.

                    *

We slip into the darkest colour – stillness.
A half-sleep floats like tempera across
our pillows and our limbs, sunk on each other,
and in the dream that blooms from our alignment,
we wake into the rosy corner where

an icon flickers, wake into the icon.
On crimson cloth, the twenty chosen fingers
enact their imperfective verbs of touch.
The child's left hand clasps the maphorion
as it would a stream of hair; his mother's cheek
touches his, and one hand curves a cradle
for the small, uncertain spine; the other, raised,
hushes the infant universe. Dissolving
to a drowse of gold, these two chosen heads,
these twenty fingers, can never say enough,
though laden with the silences of art.

*

The sun was like a diamond. Sleepily
while you worked nearby I tried to hold it
between my eyelids. All the birds were singing
to the sky's cold lavender. I slept again
letting you float — I trusted you to float
not far away. Such brightness trellised us
as if the iconographer had worked
in silver foil and gold, in pearl and turquoise.
The Virgin of the Don, like a czarina
in tear-drop gems and furry velvets, parted
the sky to smile. This was the world of money,
of purchasable grace. I woke and saw
your turned back, the diagrams spread out,
the lamp dipped as an aid to concentration
on slightly displaced, slightly obsolete fact.
Your small, plump, precise hand gripped the ruler
in its mouth, happy as a little dog.
You squinted down and drew a swift straight line.

*

But space is curved, and all who sail in her
— plasmid, bacterium, foetus, curly brain,

the sea. Deep in each other's laps we slept,
well-matched for cradling. One shall never move
without the other, that's the law of nights.
The law of days is – one shall always move
while the other gasps, writhes up, sinks back,
sick as a sturgeon ripped from its spawning-ground
and flung in pouring silver on the heaped
and blushing deck. Only the sturgeon is luckier . . .
– it makes a single mistake.
We live to lift the glass again, to chase
the flying stillness, the mortal icons.

*

In the window lay blue light and other windows;
then there was only the print of this room
on glossy black, with a bare, sickle moon
that seemed to pierce me; now, beyond the faint
kitchen glints, as far as I can see
there is only black. I could be persuaded
that no moon exists, no trees, no windows
rooted in the round earth, no hope of daylight.
Patience, patience, say the little hearth-gods
smug on your hooks and shelves, unafraid of fire
or servitude – despair is simply one
point of view. And so I try again.
I imagine you travelling beneath the moon
I cannot see, I imagine you moving slowly
into this narrow frame. A greenish dawn
follows you, then the trees, the houses, daylight.
I imagine hope, and hope's redundancy,
our dark silhouette of reunion
like an endless still that vanishes behind
the kissing curtains and the piecemeal snowfall
– after which there is nothing ever after.

*

She waited too; dawn did not bring you home.
Letters were sealed in tears, and crossed. One pleaded,
the other said — impossible. She froze . . .
The iron echo rings — impossible.
Something she'd read was happening to her:
a train pounding over the wooden bridge
over the frozen lake, and then its windows
slithering like a deck of yellowed cards
down through crashing struts, flames, slopes of ice.
The doors of the water closed. Your letters crossed,
sealed in freezing tears. Everything froze.
She stares up from the bottom of the lake.
The ice has healed smooth as lies, white-faced
as history. Impossible . . . yet you,
when I look down again, are lying there too.

*

This was my dream. You stood in the doorway,
turning the dimmer-switch to a dark glow.
I saw the smiling boy, his butterfly-pause
in the shiny perspex trap, the matted gold
curtain-weave, the junk-shop paperbacks;
then, by the bed, your blue-bound Russian–English
slavar — a daring marriage
of words solemnly trying to mean each other,
telling their secrets in each other's arms.
I woke to the old standing-pool of dawn,
seeing only myself. The light changed,
shook with a breaking tremor . . .
You were beside me. So it's possible
to be happy, I said, and, in my dream,
I took your warm, lost body to my heart
and nursed my happiness to sleep again.

*

Minutes ago we were strangers . . . Now,
expecting my surprise, you fetch the *vobla*.
Have you forgotten the first taste you fed me?
Our tongues were stiffer, salt was sweeter, then.
You gesture doubtfully, intent on stripping
the fish to a few details of its life: —
the papery, jointed pod of the swim-bladder,
still tenderly inflated, twisting free,
and now the roe, delicately male
and seaweed-brown, not red as I'd imagined.
What part of light, what part of time is this?
Age, weariness, iconoclasm
watch us for our living salts, our rich
human skins . . . we swallow the drouth
till nothing's left beyond our lips but scales.
You wouldn't eat them, though I said so once,
wanting the pun, and your dear, careful mouth.

                *

The boy, so harshly combed and tightly buttoned
into his minature pin-stripes, looks up
with sparkling gaze and vague, milk-tooth smile,
all-trusting, though a tiny flinch betrays
his sudden, bright, important loneliness.
Somewhere off-camera you are watching him,
moving farther away but watching, watching,
till your eyes bleed with their attempt at filming.
Twenty years later, and you telephone
a birthday greeting, straining to receive
across a shower of crackling stars his tall
uncertain image, and to hear him smile.

                *

There was another child, a child of wishes.
Long shadows had fallen, it was late,

but I saw him playing down by shallow water,
his language yours, diminutive, rinsed new.
For a moment, I thought you watched him too,
and the brightness in our eyes was one brightness.

   *

I am not the one.
Your fingertips understand it when they blindly
trace my short hair to a little below
the nape of my neck, no further.
I am not the one.
Still they trail onwards, smudging adored soft ghosts.
Dark, were they, or light, or in-between?
Ringlets, or straight strands?
Your finger-tips could say, but so much knowledge
cannot translate to our shadow-language, thin
as the paper I write on. Without a past
we'll die to each other, ghost to ghost . . .
Your fingers mark the stony place.
They are human enough, they search for comfort,
but go on whispering: this is not the one.

   *

Into the snowy east of consciousness
your dreams pull sledges, and your eyes are sealed
to keep the future from your wintering heart.
What's sourer than the after-taste of hope,
the nightly vodka at the wrong table,
the wrong attentive gaze? I think of those
who paid their one-way fare in useful lies,
the state turning a crass, wolfish cheek
on which a frail tear announced motherhood.
Is it freedom to forget the life you had,
or to carry it with you like neccessity?
The West, too, is full of snow and whispers,

and if it were a woman, it would say:
I had no choice but to disappoint you,
to become the cancelled myth, the ashamed silence,
a word that simply isn't in your language,
a foreign country, even to myself.

                    *

It was forbidden to destroy an icon.
Although, in time, the jewelled saints fell homesick
and dwindled smokily in mass ascensions,
their charisma remained, and only God,
sighing his aimlessness in moving water,
might wash and wash the remnant to pure nothing.

                    *

We too have left the life we dared not choose
on the vague strand where history runs in,
cold, innocent, light-fingered. 'Goodbye
until the next world,' Zhivago sighed
heroically to his mistress, but we lack
such cheerful metaphysics. Time is all
we ever had: you scarcely treasure it,
and I can only lock it like the ghost
of the present tense, into these antique rooms.
Better not to have tried to love at all,
perhaps, if this is the only world to love in,
and kinder never to have roused the child
we settled all those years ago to sleep,
if we did so merely to abandon it.